To my parents, who taught me to love the outdoors.

Pausing to take in the view from the Mazatzal Divide Trail (hike 13).

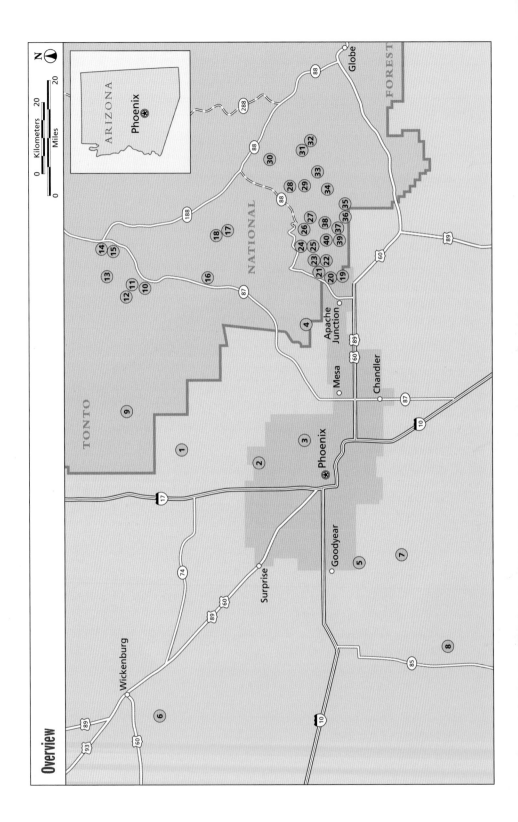

Overview

N

ARIZONA

Phoenix

Kilometers   20
0   20
0   20
Miles

Best Hikes Phoenix

The Greatest Views, Wildlife, and Desert Strolls

Second Edition

Bruce Grubbs

GUILFORD, CONNECTICUT

An imprint of The Rowman & Littlefield Publishing Group, Inc.
4501 Forbes Blvd., Ste. 200
Lanham, MD 20706
www.rowman.com
Falcon and FalconGuides are registered trademarks and Make Adventure Your Story is a trademark
of The Rowman & Littlefield Publishing Group, Inc.

Distributed by NATIONAL BOOK NETWORK

Photos by Bruce Grubbs except where indicated
Compass, p.iii, © Shutterstock
Maps by Melissa Baker

British Library Cataloguing in Publication Information available

Library of Congress Cataloging-in-Publication Data available

ISBN 978-1-4930-4787-1 (paperback)
ISBN 978-1-4930-4788-8 (e-book)

∞™ The paper used in this publication meets the minimum requirements of American National
Standard for Information Sciences—Permanence of Paper for Printed Library Materials, ANSI/NISO
Z39.48-1992.

The author and The Rowman & Littlefield Publishing Group, Inc. assume no liability for accidents
happening to, or injuries sustained by, readers who engage in the activities described in this
book.

Contents

Acknowledgments

Thank you to Stewart Aitchison, who graciously allowed me to use some of his trail descriptions. Warm thanks to Duart Martin, who patiently put up with yet another book project. And finally, thanks to my editor Emily Chiarelli, at FalconGuides for her patient efforts in making this FalconGuide a reality.

Superstition Ridges against the setting desert sun.

How to Use This Book

Each hike in the book has a number and name. Some trails have more than one common name, and some hikes use more than one trail to complete a loop or otherwise create a more interesting route. In each case, I've attempted to use either the official trail name or to give the hike a name based on the best-known trail or feature.

Each hike begins with a summary that gives a brief overview of the hike, its attractions, and location.

Start. Often the nearest town or city, this is the approximate starting point for the directions given in the Finding the trailhead description.

Distance. This is the total distance of the hike. It includes the return on an out-and-back or lollipop hike and is a one-way distance for loop hikes. A lollipop hike is one with both an out-and-back section and a loop. None of the hikes in this book require a car shuttle.

Mileages have been carefully measured with digital topo maps and may vary slightly from official and signed distances, but are consistent within the book.

Approximate hiking time. This is an average hiking time in hours for day hikes and in days for backpack trips. It is based on the total distance, the elevation gain, the condition of the trail, and the difficulty of cross-country hiking, if any. Fit, fast hikers will be able to do the hikes in less time, and inexperienced or out-of-shape hikers may take considerably more.

Elevation change. This is the approximate elevation gain or loss for the entire hike, including ups and downs. Some out-and-back hikes start from a canyon rim or other high trailhead, so that the first portion of the hike is a descent and the return is uphill.

Difficulty. All hikes are rated as easy, moderate, or strenuous. Although this is necessarily a highly subjective rating, nearly anyone who can walk should be able to do an easy hike that can be completed in a few hours. Moderate hikes are longer—up to a full day—and may involve several hundred feet or more of elevation gain and possibly cross-country hiking as well. Experienced hikers will have no problems; beginners should hike with someone more experienced and will have more fun if they are in reasonable shape. Strenuous hikes are very long, requiring a full day of hiking by fit hikers or several days, in the case of backpack trips. The hiking may involve cross-country or faint, rough trails that require good map and compass skills, and the rough terrain may require some rock scrambling. Only fit, experienced hikers should tackle these hikes.

Seasons. This section gives the best seasons for the hike, taking into account such things as winter weather and snow, as well as hot summer weather.

Trail surface. Most trails in the Phoenix region are rocky, so you should expect that. Other trail surface conditions, if known, are described here, including hikes on old roads, on paved trails, and cross-country.

Water. For backpackers (and day hikers in an emergency), known water sources are described here. Most desert springs and creeks should be considered seasonal, and you should never depend on a single source of water. All water should be purified before using it to drink or cook. Day hikers should carry all the water they'll need.

Other trail users. This is a list of the other trail users you might encounter, usually equestrians and mountain bikers.

Land status. The agency managing the land is named here; the management unit, if any, is also given.

Nearest town. This is the nearest town or city for resupply, lodging, restaurants, and other necessities.

Fees and permits. This section describes the fees and permits that are required, as well as unusual rules and regulations.

Maps. Here you'll find a list of the US Geological Survey 7.5-minute series topographic maps covering the hikes (except for very short nature trails), as well as the National Geographic Trails Illustrated map if available. The list may show national forest or wilderness maps and other privately produced maps, if useful.

Note that USGS maps as well as many others are available on web-based mapping sites such as GaiaGPS.com and CalTopo.com. These sites are very useful for trip planning.

All the hikes are shown on maps included in the book. On the maps, I give GPS coordinates in latitude/longitude (lat/long) format for the trailheads as well as occasional critical points along the route. Make certain your GPS is set to the datum used by your paper map to avoid position errors.

Trail contacts. Look here for the name of the agency or organization responsible for managing the land crossed by the hike. Detailed contact information is listed in the appendix. It's a good idea to call or e-mail the land management agency before your hike to check on road and trail conditions. Where possible, the contact information includes the mailing and street address, phone number, and Web site. E-mail addresses are not included because they often change, but you can usually find them on an agency's Web site under a "Contact" link. Sometimes Web addresses change as well, but you can find land management units on the Internet with a search engine such as Google.

Finding the trailhead. This description takes you from an obvious reference point that can be located on a street map, usually the nearest town or city, to the trailhead. Highway and road mileages were measured using digital mapping software. The GPS location of the trailhead is also shown on the trail map in lat/long. Again, be sure to set your GPS unit to the WGS84 datum.

Special considerations. This section calls your attention to specific trail hazards, like a lack of water, or warnings about when not to go (hunting seasons, ice on the trail, seasonal environmental hazards, etc.).

The Hike. Here's the meat of the hike—a detailed description of the trail or route and the features and attractions along the way. I describe the route using landmarks as well as trail signs, when possible, because trail signs can be missing. And sometimes I leave out features of the hike to preserve your sense of discovery and exploration.

Miles and Directions. This table lists the key points, such as trail intersections or turning points on a cross-country hike, by miles and tenths. You should be able to find the route with this table alone. The mileages in this book do not necessarily agree with distances found on trail signs, agency mileages, and other descriptions, because trail miles are measured by a variety of methods and personnel. All mileages were carefully measured using digital topographic mapping software for accuracy and consistency within the book.

Options. If the hike has significant options, such as side hikes, shortcuts, or extensions, you'll find the description here. Minor side hikes are described in the main hike description.

About Dogs

All the hikes in this book are in areas that allow dogs, but they must be under control. This means either leashed or under verbal command. If your dog barks or runs up to people, it is not under control and may scare other hikers.

About Wildfires

In recent years, the mountains and deserts surrounding Phoenix have suffered a number of unusually large and destructive wildfires. While fire has always been part of the natural forest ecology in Arizona, a combination of drought, invasion by exotic grasses and other plants, tree-killing insect epidemics, and overly dense forests caused by more than a century of poor management practices has led to fires burning not only hundreds of thousands of acres of forest but large areas of desert as well. A number of the hikes in this book have been affected by recent large fires, and more will be affected in the future. Always call or e-mail the relevant land management agency before you hike, or at least check its Web site for current conditions and possible area or trail closures.

Enjoy and Respect This Beautiful Landscape

As you take advantage of the spectacular scenery offered by the Phoenix area, remember that our planet is very dear, very special, and very fragile. All of us should do everything we can to keep it clean, beautiful, and healthy, including following the Green Tips you'll find throughout this book.

Introduction

It may come as a surprise that greater Phoenix, one of the most sprawling and fastest-growing cities in the world, also offers a vast array of fine hiking trails. Some of this hiking is within the many city and county parks and preserves, while many other trails and hiking routes are found in regional parks, national monuments, national forests, and other public lands surrounding the urban area.

This FalconGuide features forty hikes located in the greater Phoenix area and within approximately an hour's drive from the edges of the city. The urban area includes the city of Phoenix as well as several smaller cities including Mesa, Tempe, Scottsdale, Chandler, Apache Junction which have grown together to form greater Phoenix. Ranging from short, easy day hikes on well-traveled trails to strenuous multiday backpack trips and demanding cross-country travel, the hikes in the book offer something for every hiker—all within easy reach of the city.

Geology

In terms of geology, Arizona is one of the most diverse states. It can be divided into three physiographic (i.e., similar in geologic history) areas—the Colorado Plateau, the Central Highlands, and the Basin and Range province.

The Colorado Plateau is a region of high plateaus, deep canyons, and isolated volcanic mountains covering all of northern Arizona, about half of Utah, and portions of Colorado and New Mexico.

Stretching in a broad band across the middle of Arizona are the Central Highlands. The Highlands are a transition zone between the relatively flat-lying sedimentary rocks of the Colorado Plateau and the tortured and convoluted metamorphic and igneous rocks of the Basin and Range Country. Hikers in the Highlands find themselves in deep canyons and/or struggling up rugged mountains.

The Basin and Range Country covers southern and western Arizona and extends into western Utah, Nevada, eastern California, and northwestern Mexico. Broad desert valleys separate the numerous mountain ranges. To the west and southwest within Arizona, the small, corrugated ranges are typically dry desert all the way to their summit ridges.

Greater Phoenix lies in the Salt River Valley (dubbed the Valley of the Sun by the local chambers of commerce), a broad desert valley situated on the northeastern margin of the Basin and Range province. The mountains within the urban area—the Phoenix Mountains, South Mountain, the McDowell Mountains, and others—are typical Basin and Range mountains: low, rocky desert ranges separated by broad desert plains. More desert ranges bound the urban area to the southwest, west, and northwest, including the rugged Sierra Estrella and the Vulture Mountains. In contrast, the mountains north and east of the city are part of the Central Highlands province—these mountains rise high enough to have pine-forested summits and ridges.

Mature saguaro cactus develop arms after about 75 years and can reach 40 to 50 feet in height.

Portions of two of these ranges are featured in this book—the southern Mazatzal Mountains and the western Superstition Mountains. The Superstition Mountains in particular are a rich and complex range. The "Sups," as locals call this land of rugged canyons and cliffs, are one of the finest hiking areas in the state. Much of the Mazatzal Mountains are remote and little visited and offer more solitude than the other hiking areas. The Mazatzal Mountains are the highest mountains in the area covered by this book.

Natural History

Central Arizona is blessed with a remarkably rich and diverse collection of habitats—everything from open desert to high, forested mountains. Each of these habitats contains special plant and animal communities.

One major factor in producing this variety of habitats is the relationship between elevation and temperature. For every 1,000 feet gained, there is a corresponding drop of about 5 degrees Fahrenheit. Additionally, going higher usually means greater precipitation. In central Arizona, elevations range from about 900 feet above sea level in the desert valleys west of Phoenix to over 7,600 feet at the summit of Browns Peak in the southern Mazatzal Mountains.

The sun shines 85 to 90 percent of the daytime in the lower desert and only slightly less in the high country. Arizona annual temperature extremes have spanned more than 160 degrees, from a low of −37 degrees at Maverick, in the White Mountains, to a high of 127 degrees at Parker, along the Colorado River. Although the Phoenix area gets nearly as hot—the Phoenix record high is 122 degrees—the highest summits rarely fall to zero, even in midwinter. Because the air is typically very dry, the daily range of temperatures often exceeds 40 degrees. The low humidity allows daytime heat to quickly dissipate at night.

The annual precipitation can vary from nearly zero in some of the desert areas to more than 26 inches on the higher mountains. Generally, the moisture comes during one of two rainy seasons—either in the winter or late summer. At higher elevations (those above 5,000 feet), the winter precipitation mostly falls as snow.

Summer rains usually come as afternoon thundershowers, which, although generally brief, may result in heavy runoff and flash floods because of the rocky, impenetrable nature of the ground.

All of these major environmental factors, along with minor others, set the stage for the striking array of life in the state. Central Arizona contains five major biotic communities: (1) coniferous forests (7,600–6,000 feet), (2) woodlands (7,000–4,000 feet), (3) chaparral (6,000–4,000 feet), (4) grasslands (7,000–4,000 feet), and (5) deserts (4,000–900 feet).

Human History

Arizona's first human inhabitants were Paleo-hunters, who arrived at least 13,000 years ago in the waning years of the last glacial period. Arizona's weather then was considerably cooler and wetter than today, and small glaciers graced the summits of the state's highest mountains, the San Francisco Peaks and the White Mountains.

Using a spear-throwing device called an atlatl, these hunters stalked mammoth, ground sloth, giant bison, Harrington's mountain goat, tapirs (piglike mammals), cameloids, and other survivors of the Pleistocene or Glacial Epoch. Several thousands of years of gradual warming and drying decimated these great ice age mammals, and they finally disappeared. The hunters then turned their attention to other game, like deer, elk, bighorn sheep, pronghorn antelope, rabbits, squirrels and other rodents, and birds. A greater emphasis was also placed on the gathering of wild plant foods. These people had to be opportunists to survive in this unforgiving environment.

Although maize and squash were introduced into Arizona from Mexico perhaps as long as 4,000 years ago, not until about 2,000 years later did the hunter-gatherers become serious farmers. As agriculturalists, they tended to remain in one area to work and guard their small farming plots. The permanent homes they constructed were usually pit houses, partly subterranean structures with vertical poles running around the perimeter of the hole to support a roof. Later they replaced these pit houses with aboveground stone-and-mud houses, some with attached rooms and several stories high. A few dwellings were located in south-facing caves or on hilltops.

Around AD 600, people to the south in Mexico introduced Arizona's natives to beans—pinto, lima, and tepary—as well as the technique of pottery making and use of the bow and arrow. These new foods, ways of preparing them, and more efficient hunting implements apparently allowed the population to increase dramatically.

Three major and distinct Indian cultures developed along with a number of smaller groups. People in the central and southern parts of the state, whom the archaeologists call the Hohokam, engineered complex irrigation canals to carry river water onto the hot, desert plains. Some of the modern canals that cross the Salt River Valley follow the routes of the ancient canals. The Mogollon people lived in the Central Highlands and practiced both irrigation and dry farming.

By the mid-1400s, the Mogollon and Hohokam people had abandoned their villages. What caused their departure is not fully understood but was probably a combination of drought, overuse of natural resources, overpopulation, and perhaps disease and warfare.

Where did everybody go? Some probably moved out of the Arizona region entirely, while others resumed a hunting-and-gathering lifestyle. A few probably found different locations favorable to their dry-farming methods and continued their agricultural tradition. Also at about this same time, new people from the north entered the American Southwest, including the Navajo and Apache.

Arizona's historic period began in 1539 with Estéban, a black Moor, who was with the Spaniard Fray Marcos de Niza exploring north toward the American Southwest. Estéban had gone ahead of the padre and sent back word of "seven very great cities." Unfortunately, Zuni Indians killed Estéban. Hearing this news, Niza retreated to Mexico. Niza's report of a collection of cities of unbelievable riches led Francisco Vásquez de Coronado to mount an expedition the next year to find the Seven Cities of Cíbola. The Spaniards were disappointed to discover that legendary Cíbola was in reality the stone and mud pueblos of the Zuni. However, a small detachment of Coronado's men, led by García López de Cárdenas, is credited with being the first

The moon rises over rugged crags in upper Fish Creek Canyon (hike 29).

Europeans to see the Grand Canyon. Not long after this foray came Spanish padres seeking Indian souls instead of gold. Some Native Americans fared better than others under the Spanish invasion.

By the 1820s, fur trappers such as James Ohio Pattie, Jedediah Smith, Bill Williams, Pauline Weaver, and Kit Carson were traipsing along Arizona's streams and rivers even though the land was under Spanish and, after 1821, Mexican rule. After the Mexican-American War of 1847–48, Arizona and much of the Southwest became part of United States. Within a few years, prospectors, ranchers, and settlers followed, displacing the original residents—the Native Americans.

Conflict erupted as these different groups fought over Arizona's limited natural resources. However, by the end of the nineteenth century, the Old West was quickly becoming a memory. On Valentine's Day 1912, Arizona became the nation's forty-eighth state.

Still, the new state was slow to grow. Rugged terrain, hot summer weather, and difficult travel away from the railroad lines discouraged people from moving to the Southwest. However, with the start of America's involvement in World War II, the military came to the Arizona deserts to train aviators, taking advantage of the clear weather. Defense industries followed, and after the war the growth continued as people discovered the advantages of the desert climate. Widespread adoption of air-conditioning made central Arizona a pleasant place to live year-round, not just in the winter. Today Arizona is one of the fastest-growing states, with most of the state's 7 million people living in the greater Phoenix area.

Preserving Arizona's Archaeological and Historic Heritage

Arizona is fortunate to have some of the best-preserved prehistoric structures and artifacts in the world. Unfortunately, many of these sites have been vandalized to some degree. Disturbing archaeological sites or collecting artifacts not only lessens their scientific value but also deeply upsets Native Americans whose ancestors left these things behind.

Two federal laws, the American Antiquities Act and the Archaeological Resources Protection Act, forbid removal or destruction of archaeological and historical resources on federal land. The Arizona State Antiquities Act provides similar protection on state lands. Failure to comply with these laws can result in stiff fines and imprisonment, not to mention many years of bad luck and terrible nightmares inflicted by ancient spirits. Any vandalism should be immediately reported to the nearest federal or state resource office or law enforcement agency.

Map Legend

Municipal

≡(17)≡ Interstate Highway

≡(60)≡ US Highway

≡(188)≡ State Highway

≡⟨3N06⟩≡ Local Road

= = = = Unpaved Road

= = = = Unimproved Road

•—•—•—• Power Line

Trails

------ Featured Trail

------ Trail

·········· Featured Cross-country Route

·········· Cross-country Route

Water Features

Lake/Reservoir

River/Creek

Intermittent Stream

Spring

Symbols

≍ Bridge

▲ Campground

× Elevation

≍ Gap/Saddle

🅿 Parking

▲ Peak

🖽 Picnic Area

■ Point of Interest/Structure

🚻 Ranger Station

🚻 Restrooms

○ Town

① Trailhead

🔲 Viewpoint/Overlook

🏙 Windmill

Land Management

National Forest

Preserve

Regional Park

Trail Finder

Hike No.	Hike Name	Easy Day Hikes	Hikes with Children	Long Day Hikes	Hikes for Photographers	Hikes with Side Trips or Exploring	Hikes for Peak Baggers	First Night in the Wilderness	Hikes for Backpackers
1	Go John Trail	•	•						
2	Lookout Mountain	•	•				•		
3	Echo Canyon Trail	•			•		•		
4	Pass Mountain Trail				•				
5	Baseline Trail	•	•						
6	Vulture Peak			•	•		•		
7	Quartz Peak Trail			•					
8	Margies Cove Trail			•		•			
9	Cave Creek Trail			•	•	•			
10	Marion Spring			•		•			
11	Squaw Flat			•		•			
12	Copper Camp Canyon			•	•	•			
13	Mazatzal Divide Trail			•	•	•	•		
14	Deer Creek			•		•		•	
15	South Fork of Deer Creek			•		•		•	
16	Camp Creek			•		•			
17	Browns Peak				•		•		
18	Pigeon Spring Loop	•	•		•				
19	Western Foothills		•		•				

#	Trail	1	2	3	4	5	6	7	8
20	Siphon Draw			●	●	●	●		
21	Massacre Grounds					●		●	●
22	Garden Valley Loop				●	●	●		
23	Second Water Trail				●	●	●		
24	Lower La Barge Box		●			●	●		
25	Marsh Valley Loop	●	●		●	●			
26	Peters Mesa	●			●	●			
27	Tortilla Pass–Red Tanks Divide	●			●	●			
28	Reavis Ranch	●	●						
29	Upper Fish Creek	●			●	●			
30	Pinyon Mountain			●	●	●	●		
31	Fireline Loop			●	●	●			
32	Mountain Spring						●		
33	Reavis Creek	●				●			
34	Angel Basin	●			●	●			
35	Randolph Canyon						●		
36	Coffee Flat Mountain Loop	●	●			●			
37	Bluff Spring Loop	●				●	●		
38	Dutchmans Loop	●	●			●			
39	Barks Canyon					●	●		
40	Needle Canyon				●	●	●		

Chainfruit cholla and saguaro cactus symbolize the Phoenix area.

Greater Phoenix

I solated desert mountain ranges and desert hills are spotted throughout the greater Phoenix area, and many are preserved as city or county parks that provide trails for hikers. These trails range from short, easy walks to longer loop hikes. Because all of these hikes lie at low elevations in the desert, they are scorchingly hot in the summer. Hot-season hikes should be made early in the day, starting at sunrise, and you must have at least one gallon of water per person. On the other hand, the winter months offer cool and pleasant hiking weather, and spring and fall are also a delight.

1 Go John Trail

This trail winds through the lush Sonoran Desert foothills near Cave Creek, north of Phoenix. The first part of the loop follows an old road dating from the prospecting and mining era of the nineteenth century. After crossing a pass, the pleasant foot trail traverses the north side of some low hills, providing views north to the remote New River Mountains area. There are also good views of the Cave Creek area and the McDowell Mountains.

Start: Just west of Cave Creek
Distance: 4.8-mile loop
Approximate hiking time: 2 hours
Elevation change: 300 feet
Difficulty: Easy due to short distance, good trails, and little elevation change
Seasons: Fall through spring
Trail surface: Dirt and rocks

Water: None
Other trail users: Mountain bikes and horses
Land status: Cave Creek Regional Park
Nearest town: Cave Creek
Fees and permits: Park entrance fee
Map: USGS Cave Creek
Trail contact: Maricopa County Parks and Recreation

Finding the trailhead: From Interstate 17, drive east on Carefree Highway to 32nd Street. Turn north and go into the Cave Creek Regional Park. Pass the horse rental and picnic areas, and then turn left at the second trailhead sign. The Go John Trail is signed. GPS: N33 49.945' W112 0.066'

The Hike

This pleasant loop gives hikers a good introduction to the Sonoran Desert. From the trailhead, the Go John Trail first heads north up a drainage, climbing to a low saddle in the desert hills. It then drops north down a dry wash. As the trail turns east, watch for unmarked unofficial trails that leave the park; stay right, on the Go John Trail, at each junction. The trail crosses several minor drainages as it skirts the base of the hills on their north slopes. It then turns south and climbs gradually over another low saddle. Turning east again, the Go John Trail descends a drainage, then turns southwest around the end of a ridge, where it starts to climb again. It crosses a third saddle before turning west and descending along the south slopes of the hills to return to the trailhead.
—Stewart Aitchison and Bruce Grubbs

GREEN TIP
Carpool or take public transportation to the trailhead.

Young saguaro cactus are common along the Go John Trail in Cave Creek Regional Park.

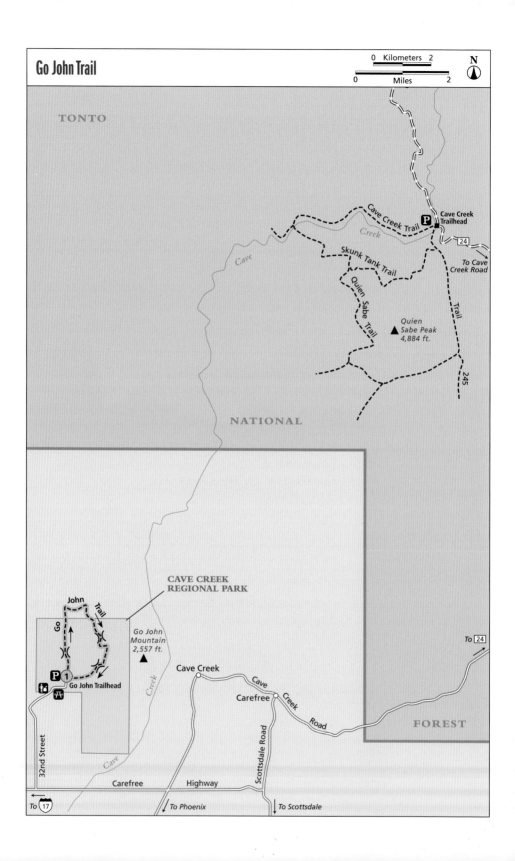

Go John Trail

0 Kilometers 2

0 Miles 2

N

TONTO

Cave Creek Trail

Cave Creek Trailhead

P

24

To Cave Creek Road

Skunk Tank Trail

Quien Sabe Trail

Creek

Cave

Quien Sabe Peak 4,884 ft.

Trail

245

NATIONAL

CAVE CREEK REGIONAL PARK

John

Go

Trail

Go John Mountain 2,557 ft.

P

1

Go John Trailhead

Cave

Cave Creek

Carefree

Cave

Creek

Road

To 24

FOREST

32nd Street

Scottsdale Road

Cave

Carefree

Highway

To 17

To Phoenix

To Scottsdale

Brilliant orange globemallow often graces the Sonoran Desert after plentiful winter rains.

Miles and Directions

0.0	Begin at Go John Trailhead.
2.0	Watch for unofficial trails; stay right at each junction.
4.8	Return to Go John Trailhead.

DUAL RAINY SEASONS SUPPORT SONORAN PLANTS

The abundance and diversity of desert plant life surprises most first-time visitors. One factor that allows the Sonoran Desert to contain so many different kinds of plants—from cacti to small trees to shrubs to wildflowers—is that there are two rainy seasons, the first during December through March and the second in late July. Certain plants tend to utilize the winter moisture, while other species tend to rely upon the summer rains. Thus, not every plant is competing all the time with its neighbor for the precious, rare fluid.

2 Lookout Mountain

An easily accessible walk around a prominent hill in the Sonoran Desert, this trail provides a 360-degree view of the northern suburbs of Phoenix. Though you're still near those suburbs, it doesn't feel like it, and you can easily imagine the time, not so long ago, when this was all open desert. Keep an eye out for coyotes. You might also spot typical desert birds such as roadrunners or Gila woodpeckers. For those who want a little longer hike, a spur trail leads to the top of Lookout Mountain.

Start: North Phoenix
Distance: 1.8-mile loop
Approximate hiking time: 1 hour
Elevation change: 400 feet on main trail; 470 feet to summit of Lookout Mountain
Difficulty: Easy due to short distance, good trails, and little elevation change
Seasons: Fall through spring
Trail surface: Dirt and rocks

Water: None
Other trail users: None
Land status: Phoenix Mountains Preserve
Nearest town: Phoenix
Fees and permits: None
Map: USGS Union Hills and Sunnyslope
Trail contact: City of Phoenix

Finding the trailhead: From Bell Road, drive south about 1 mile on 16th Street to the Lookout Mountain park entrance. The trailhead is at the parking area. GPS: N33 37.624' W112 2.893'

The Hike

The Circumference Trail goes around Lookout Mountain and can be hiked in either direction. If you want to go counterclockwise, start on the Summit Trail at the right (west) side of the parking lot. After 0.1 mile, turn right onto the Circumference Trail. The trail climbs across the open Sonoran Desert slope and loops around a smaller hill before passing through a saddle. The trail now descends across the south slopes of Lookout Mountain. There are numerous side trails that branch right to trailheads on private land; stay left at all these junctions. After the trail passes along the east side of the mountain, it climbs over a ridge and then descends to the Lookout Mountain Trailhead.
—Stewart Aitchison and Bruce Grubbs

Barrel cactus dot the rocky slopes below Lookout Mountain. ▶

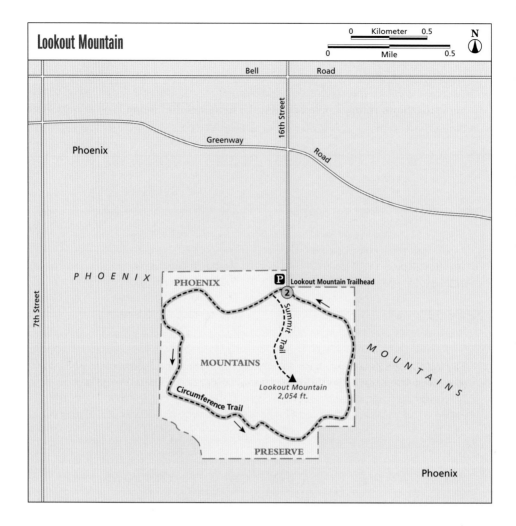

Miles and Directions

0.0 Begin at Lookout Mountain Trailhead.

0.1 Summit Trail junction; turn right.

1.8 Return to Lookout Mountain Trailhead.

Option

About 0.1 mile after the start, turn left on the Summit Trail for a 0.6-mile climb to the top of Lookout Mountain and a 360-degree view of the Valley of the Sun.

3 Echo Canyon Trail

Camelback Mountain is the defining landmark of Phoenix and the Valley of the Sun. This trail starts on the north side of the "camel's head," traverses below some towering cliffs, climbs to the saddle between the head and the "hump," and then runs up the west ridge of the camel's hump to the highest point on the mountain. Because this scenic trail is in the middle of the urban area, it is very popular, and the parking lot fills quickly on weekend mornings. Your best chance at a parking spot is to hike early on a weekday.

Start: On the Phoenix-Paradise Valley border
Distance: 2.0 miles out and back
Approximate hiking time: 2 hours
Elevation change: 1,000 feet
Difficulty: Easy due to short distance, good trails, and moderate elevation change
Seasons: Fall through spring
Trail surface: Dirt and rocks

Water: None
Other trail users: None
Land status: City of Phoenix
Nearest town: Phoenix
Fees and permits: None
Map: USGS Paradise Valley
Trail contact: City of Phoenix

Finding the trailhead: From North 44th Street at East Camelback Road in northeast Phoenix, go north on 44th Street. Follow the curve to the right onto East McDonald Drive. At Tatum Road (traffic light), turn right to remain on East McDonald Drive, then almost immediately turn right into Echo Canyon Trailhead. On weekends, the parking lot fills quickly. GPS: N33 31.406' W111 58.475'

The Hike

The popular but spectacular Echo Canyon Trail climbs southeast through a saddle, then ascends below a dramatic line of cliffs to the saddle between the camel's head and camel's hump. The trail then more or less follows the west ridge of Camelback Mountain to the hump—the summit. On clear days, the view of the Valley of the Sun is simply stunning.

GREEN TIP

When hiking with your dog, stay in the center of the path and keep Fido close by. Dogs that run loose can harm fragile soils and spread pesky plants by carrying their seeds.

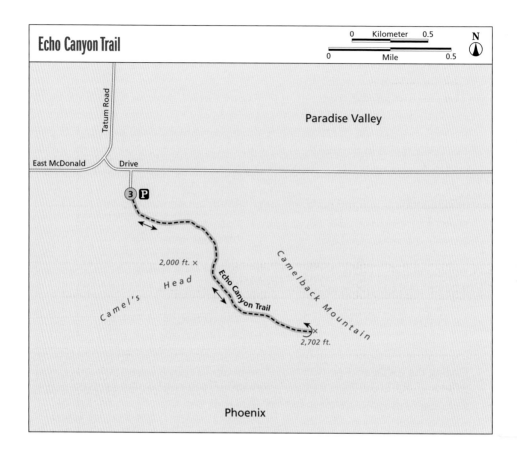

SAVING THE PHOENIX SKYLINE

As you look around from the summit, it's clear that Phoenicians love to build expensive houses on steep hillsides. In fact, in the 1970s the privately owned summit of Camelback Mountain was slated to have the top 300 feet blasted off to make room for a restaurant. This was too much for citizens who were losing the distinctive desert skyline of the city to the scars of roads on steep mountainsides and buildings on ridge crests. Concerted effort led the City of Phoenix to buy much of the remaining undeveloped portion of Camelback as a park. Similar efforts resulted in the creation of a preserve for much of the remaining undeveloped Phoenix Mountains to the northwest of Camelback Mountain.

Miles and Directions

0.0 Begin at Echo Canyon Trailhead.

1.0 Reach summit.

2.0 Return to trailhead.

The Echo Canyon Trail ascends along the base of the yellow cliff, then climbs the right-hand skyline of Camelback Mountain.

4 Pass Mountain Trail

This trail starts in the Usery Mountain Regional Park, then spends most of its time in the Tonto National Forest, looping through the western Goldfield Mountains northeast of Mesa. It offers a fine sense of remoteness, considering its location near the greater Phoenix area. Once on the east side of Pass Mountain, you'll be looking north and east toward three wilderness areas within a few dozen miles of the metropolitan area. After wet winters, this is a fine place to see desert wildflowers.

Start: North Mesa
Distance: 7.7-mile loop
Approximate hiking time: 4 hours
Elevation change: 950 feet
Difficulty: Moderate due to distance and elevation change
Seasons: Fall through spring
Trail surface: Dirt and rocks
Water: None

Other trail users: Mountain bikes and horses
Land status: Usery Mountain Regional Park, Tonto National Forest
Nearest town: Mesa
Fees and permits: Park entrance fee
Maps: USGS, Apache Junction; Trails Illustrated Superstition and Four Peaks Wildernesses; Usery Mountain Regional Park map
Trail contact: Usery Mountain Regional Park

Finding the trailhead: From Mesa, go north on Ellsworth Road, which becomes Usery Pass Road. Turn right at the park entrance and go to the horse-staging area, which is the trailhead. GPS: N33 28.436' W111 36.434'

The Hike

A couple hundred yards from the start, turn left at a T intersection to begin the loop. The trail wanders north along the east side of the park facilities. After passing a final ramada and parking area, you'll pass Wind Cave Trail; stay left. The trail works its way north along the west slopes of Pass Mountain. A fence marks the boundary of Tonto National Forest. Now the trail climbs gradually around the north side of the mountain. As it crosses a ridge, the remainder of the Goldfield Mountains becomes visible to the northeast and, beyond, the Four Peaks, the Mazatzal Mountains, and the Superstition Mountains. Rich Sonoran Desert foothills offer open views with classic desert vegetation, such as saguaro and cholla cactus, in the foreground. Continuing to climb, the trail turns south into a canyon and climbs to a pass. This is the high point of the hike. With the bulk of Pass Mountain hiding the metropolitan area to the southwest, this saddle is a wild and rugged spot.

The trail descends north from the saddle via a switchback, then works its way south along the foot of the mountain. As you reach the mouth of the canyon and the southern foothills, the trail starts to swing west along the base of the mountain. Ignore an unsigned trail branching left, and stay right at the junction with the Cat

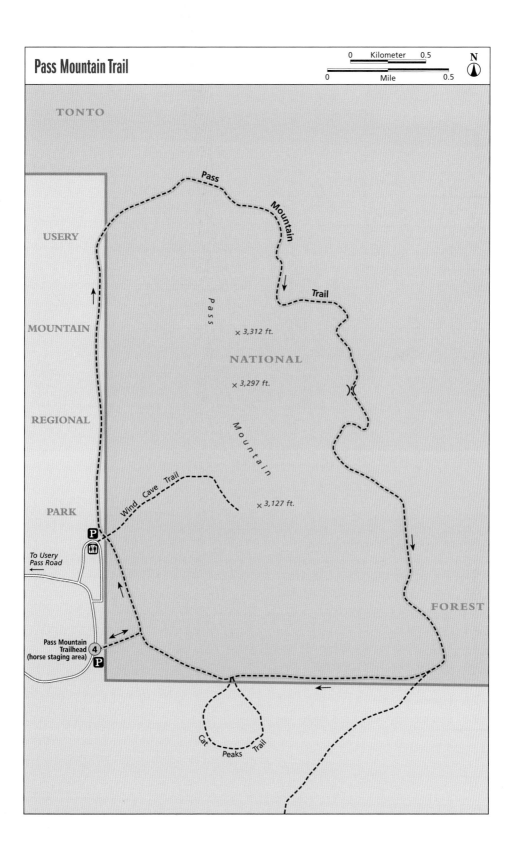

Pass Mountain Trail

TONTO

USERY

MOUNTAIN

REGIONAL

PARK

To Usery
Pass Road

Pass Mountain
Trailhead (4)
(horse staging area)

Pass

Mountain

Trail

Pass

× 3,312 ft.

NATIONAL

× 3,297 ft.

Mountain

Wind Cave Trail

× 3,127 ft.

FOREST

Cat Peaks Trail

0   Kilometer   0.5

0   Mile   0.5

N

Teddybear cholla cactus "garden" grows on the slopes below Pass Mountain.

Peaks Trail. When you reach the T intersection near the horse-staging area, turn left to return to the trailhead.

Miles and Directions

0.0 Start at horse-staging area; head east on Pass Mountain Trail; turn left at T intersection.

0.7 Stay left at junction with Wind Cave Trail.

2.3 Cross into Tonto National Forest.

4.4 Reach pass.

4.6 Old trail forks left; stay right on new trail.

6.1 Unsigned trail junction; stay right.

7.1 Cat Peaks Trail junction; stay right.

7.6 T intersection; turn left.

7.7 Return to trailhead at horse-staging area.

5 Baseline Trail

An easy day hike in the Sonoran Desert foothills on the north end of the Sierra Estrella, this loop trail makes a good introduction to the trail system in Estrella Mountain Regional Park. It is less crowded than the better-known trails in the city and is also an ideal trail for beginning hikers and even nonhikers.

Start: About 25 miles west of Phoenix
Distance: 2.1-mile loop
Approximate hiking time: 1 hour
Elevation change: 200 feet
Difficulty: Easy due to short distance and little elevation change
Seasons: Fall through spring
Trail surface: Dirt and rocks
Water: None

Other trail users: None
Land status: Estrella Mountain Regional Park
Nearest town: Phoenix
Fees and permits: Park entrance fee
Maps: USGS Perryville, Tolleson, Avondale SE, and Avondale SW; park map
Trail contact: Maricopa County Parks and Recreation

Finding the trailhead: From Phoenix, drive west on Interstate 10 about 25 miles to the Estrella Parkway exit. Go south 7 miles, then turn left onto Vineyard Road. Go about 2.5 miles to the Estrella Mountain Regional Park entrance. Pick up a park trail map here. Now follow Casey Abbott Drive North and 143rd Drive to the first signed trailhead on the right. GPS: N33 22.909' W112 22.200'

The Hike

Start on the signed Gila Trail, a barrier-free interpretive loop. Stay left and follow the Gila Trail clockwise to a ramada. Turn left here onto the Baseline Trail, which gradually climbs southwest up the left side of a ravine to another junction. Stay left here—the right fork will be the return from the Baseline Trail loop portion of the hike. Climbing gradually, the Baseline Trail continues over a saddle, then contours around the south slopes of the peak. Several trails branch left toward the horse-staging area, visible to the south. Stay right at all these junctions.

The view includes the northern end of the rugged Sierra Estrella. As the trail loops around a small peak, you'll pass through typical low-elevation Sonoran Desert,

NEST, SWEET NEST

Look for football-size cactus wren nests in the abundant cholla cacti. The nest's interior is accessible only through a small opening at one end. The cactus wren is North America's largest wren at 8 to 9 inches in length. Unlike most birds, this wren can be heard singing year-round.

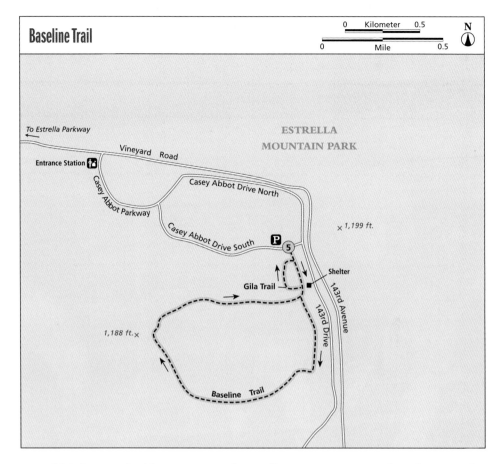

0   Kilometer   0.5

N

0   Mile   0.5

To Estrella Parkway

ESTRELLA

MOUNTAIN PARK

Vineyard   Road

Entrance Station

Casey Abbot Drive North

Casey Abbot Parkway

Casey Abbot Drive South

× 1,199 ft.

5

Shelter

Gila Trail →

143rd Avenue

143rd Drive

1,188 ft. ×

Baseline   Trail

which is covered with sparse vegetation—tall saguaro cactus, squat barrel cactus, spin-dly staghorn cholla cactus, and creosote bushes.

After the Baseline Trail crosses the north slopes, it descends into a ravine to meet the start of the loop. Turn left here and walk northeast a short distance to the ramada on the Gila Trail. Turn left to return to the trailhead.—Bruce Grubbs and Stewart Aitchison

Miles and Directions

0.0 Begin at Gila Trailhead.

0.2 Baseline Trail junction at ramada; turn left.

0.3 Baseline Trail loop; stay left.

1.8 End of Baseline Trail loop; turn left.

1.9 Baseline Trail junction at ramada; turn left.

2.1 Return to Gila Trailhead.

A lone saguaro cactus stands sentinel along the Baseline Trail in Estrella Mountain Regional Park.

Desert Ranges

For hikes in a more remote setting, take to the numerous low desert mountain ranges that lie generally southwest through northwest from the Phoenix area. Summer is definitely not the prime hiking season here due to daytime temperatures that often exceed 110 degrees, but spring and fall are usually balmy, and winter days are cool but pleasant. Lying south of Wickenburg, the Vulture Mountains are a low range of desert hills punctuated by the domelike, cliff-bound summit of Vulture Peak. Southwest of the greater Phoenix area lies the Sierra Estrella, a long, exceptionally rugged and remote 5,000-foot range. West of the city, the Maricopas offer easy trails through low but classic Sonoran Desert mountains in a largely untouched wilderness. North of the metropolitan complex, the New River Mountains provide hikers with a more complex terrain and even some live streams.

Ocotillo blooms after desert rains.

Prickly pear cactus fruit served as a food source for native Americans and is still made into jelly today.

6 Vulture Peak

Vulture Peak is a distinctive landmark southwest of Wickenburg, noted for its dome-like summit and steep, east-facing cliffs. This trail leads through the gorgeous Sonoran Desert foothills on the west side of the mountain and up to Vulture Saddle. A short scramble leads to the summit, where you'll have views of the surrounding Vulture Mountains, as well as the distant Harquahala, Hieroglyphic, Bradshaw, Big Horn, and Eagletail Mountains. It's an unforgettable vista of the open desert north and west of Phoenix.

Start: About 40 miles northwest of Phoenix
Distance: 4.0 miles out and back
Approximate hiking time: 3 hours
Elevation change: 1,180 feet
Difficulty: Moderate due to elevation change and rock scramble at end
Seasons: Fall through spring
Trail surface: Dirt and rocks

Water: None
Other trail users: None
Land status: Bureau of Land Management
Nearest town: Wickenburg
Fees and permits: None
Map: USGS Vulture Peak
Trail contact: Phoenix Field Office, Bureau of Land Management

Finding the trailhead: From Phoenix, drive about 30 miles northwest on U.S. Highway 60 to Wickenburg, then drive south 7 miles on Vulture Mine Road. About 0.7 mile past milepost 30, turn left onto the signed Vulture Peak Trail Road. It's another 0.4 mile to the trailhead parking area. GPS: N33 52.636' W112 49.043'

The Hike

The trail winds through the wonderful Sonoran Desert. Saguaro, ocotillo, palo verde, jojoba, creosote bush, teddybear cholla, and staghorn cholla hug the trail. The first 1.6 miles or so make for a fairly gradual climb; then you meet the end of the four-wheel-drive road, and the trail begins to ascend more

SKY LIFE

Look for black-throated sparrows, North America's only desert bird that does not have to drink water. It gets moisture from metabolizing the carbohydrates, fats, and proteins in the seeds that it eats. Keep an eye out, too, for the delicate silky flycatchers known as phainopeplas, which feed on mistletoe berries in the palo verde trees. You might also spot some Say's phoebes "hawking" insects out of the air.

The moon rises above Vulture Peak. ▶

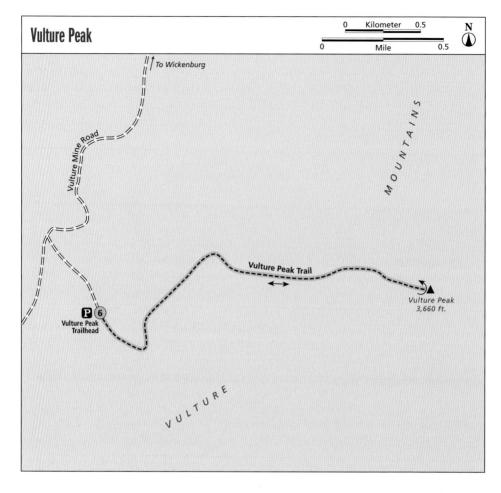

steeply. Take your time, enjoy the views, and before long you will reach Vulture Saddle. There are grand vistas from here, but if you have a little more energy, it's only another 240-vertical-foot scramble to the summit of Vulture Peak.
—Stewart Aitchison

Miles and Directions

0.0 Begin at trailhead.

1.9 Arrive at Vulture Saddle.

2.0 Reach Vulture Peak.

4.0 Retrace your steps to trailhead.

7 Quartz Peak Trail

This unique trail climbs to a summit along the crest of the Sierra Estrella. Reaching over 4,500 feet, the Sierra Estrella forms the southwestern skyline of the Valley of the Sun. On this hike, you'll climb a scenic desert ridge to a sharp summit that provides views of much of southwestern Arizona, including the Eagletail Mountains to the west, the White Tank Mountains to the north, South Mountain to the east, and countless Sonoran Desert ranges to the south. The trail lies in the Sierra Estrella Wilderness.

Start: About 20 miles southwest of Phoenix
Distance: 6.0 miles out and back
Approximate hiking time: 5 hours
Elevation change: 2,502 feet
Difficulty: Strenuous due to steep, rough trail and final scramble to summit
Seasons: Fall through spring
Trail surface: Dirt and rocks, boulders and talus near summit

Water: None
Other trail users: None
Land status: Sierra Estrella Wilderness, Bureau of Land Management
Nearest town: Phoenix
Fees and permits: None
Map: USGS Montezuma Peak
Trail contacts: Phoenix Field Office, Bureau of Land Management

Finding the trailhead: Although distinguished for its close proximity to metropolitan Phoenix, the Sierra Estrella Wilderness is inaccessible without a four-wheel-drive vehicle. Primitive dirt roads near the wilderness boundary are extremely sandy or silty, and wash crossings are rugged and deep. Take Interstate 10 to exit 126 and travel 8.3 miles south to Elliot Road. Turn right and go 2.6 miles to Rainbow Valley Road. Turn left and drive 9.3 miles south until the pavement ends. Turn left onto Riggs Road; continue 4.0 miles to an intersection, then go straight another 5.3 miles to a power line road. Turn right and drive 1.9 miles to a road to the left. Take it 1.9 miles east to the Quartz Peak Trailhead. Some lands around and within the wilderness are not federally administered. Please respect the property rights of the owners, and do not cross or use these lands without their permission. GPS: N33 11.936' W112 14.400'

The Hike

Quartz Peak Trail, in the 14,400-acre Sierra Estrella Wilderness, leads visitors from the floor of Rainbow Valley (elevation 1,550 feet) to the summit ridge of the Sierra Estrella at Quartz Peak (elevation 4,052 feet) in just 3 miles. The trail is extremely steep and difficult to follow in places. Granite boulder–strewn terrain also makes cross-country hiking in the Estrella difficult, and there are few trails. This is a hike for experienced and well-conditioned hikers only!

Next page: Stately saguaro cactus can be found below Quartz Peak, in the Sierra Estrella.

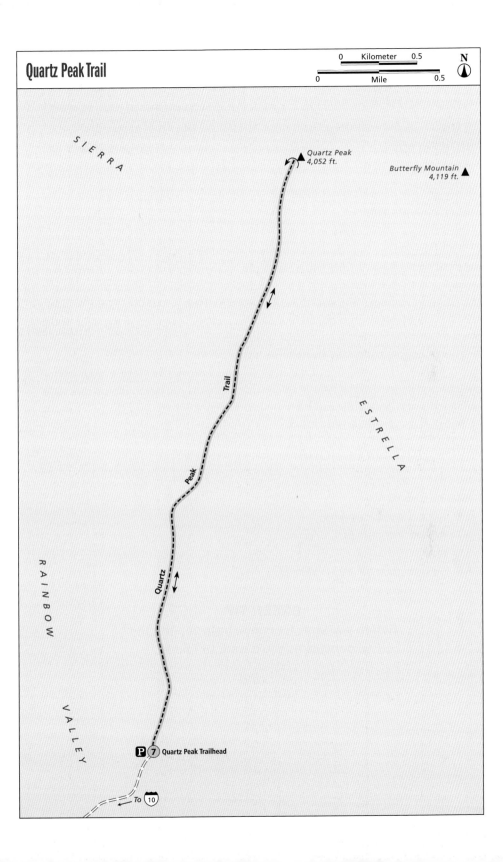

Quartz Peak Trail

0　　　Kilometer　0.5

0　　　Mile　0.5

N

SIERRA

Quartz Peak
4,052 ft.

Butterfly Mountain
4,119 ft.

ESTRELLA

Trail

Peak

RAINBOW

Quartz

VALLEY

P 7 Quartz Peak Trailhead

To 10

SONORAN DESERT IS ANYTHING BUT DESERTED

The landscape of the North Maricopas is a jumble of long ridges and isolated peaks separated by extensive, saguaro-studded outwash plains (bajadas) and wide desert washes. Cholla, ocotillo, prickly pear, palo verde, ironwood, and Mexican jumping bean complement the thick stands of saguaro to form classic Sonoran Desert vistas. Commonly seen wildlife include desert mule deer, javelina, desert bighorn sheep, coyote, desert tortoise, and numerous varieties of lizards and birds.

From the Quartz Peak Trailhead, follow a closed four-wheel-drive track approximately 0.3 mile. Look to the left as you walk up the old road to find a narrow trail ascending the ridge to the north. The trail is poorly marked in places and does not extend to the summit—the final 0.3 mile to Quartz Peak is a scramble over boulders and talus slopes that require careful footing. Quartz Peak is a point on the spine of the Sierra Estrella capped by an outcrop of white quartz.

Along the way visitors are treated to a variety of Sonoran Desert plants and wildlife, scenic vistas, and evidence of the area's volcanic history. The views from the summit are spectacular—to the west is a dramatic panorama of rugged mountain ranges and desert plains, and to the east metropolitan Phoenix unfolds over the valley of the lower Salt River.—Stewart Aitchison

Miles and Directions

- **0.0** Begin at trailhead.
- **0.4** Trail starts up ridge.
- **1.7** Grade moderates somewhat.
- **2.7** Trail ends; begin scramble to summit.
- **3.0** Arrive at Quartz Peak.
- **6.0** Follow the same trail back to trailhead.

GREEN TIP
Before you start for home, have you left the
wilderness as you'd want to find it?

8 Margies Cove Trail

Both the South and North Maricopa Mountains are within wilderness areas. Separated only by a railroad corridor, both are encompassed within the Sonoran Desert National Monument. This hike takes you across Sonoran Desert plains into a scenic canyon in the North Maricopa Mountains. You'll see man-made attractions on this hike too, such as relics from the prospecting and ranching days.

Start: About 50 miles southwest of Phoenix
Distance: 10.4 miles out and back
Approximate hiking time: 5 hours
Elevation change: 700 feet
Difficulty: Moderate due to distance
Seasons: Fall through spring
Trail surface: Dirt and rocks
Water: None

Other trail users: Horses
Land status: North Maricopa Mountains Wilderness, Sonoran Desert National Monument, Bureau of Land Management
Nearest town: Phoenix
Fees and permits: None
Map: USGS Cotton Center SE
Trail contact: Phoenix Field Office, Bureau of Land Management

Finding the trailhead: From Phoenix drive about 30 miles west on I-10, then exit south on Highway 85. Drive about 21 miles south and exit at Woods Road. Turn left, cross the overpass, and turn left again onto the frontage road. Drive north about 1 mile to reach the Margies Cove Road; turn right (east). After 4 miles, turn right (south) and continue 1.6 miles to the Margies Cove West Trailhead. These dirt roads are passable to cars if driven with care. GPS: N33 7.54' W112 34.92'

Lines of mesquite trees mark dry washes near the Margies Cove Trail, in the North Maricopa Mountains.

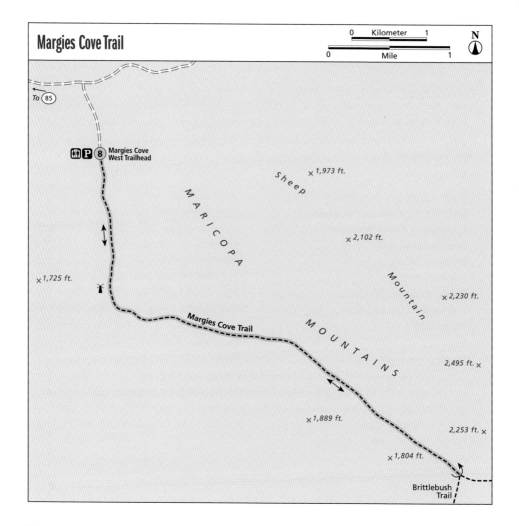

Margies Cove Trail

0   Kilometer   1

0   Mile   1

N

To 85

Margies Cove
West Trailhead

Sheep

× 1,973 ft.

MARICOPA

× 2,102 ft.

× 1,725 ft.

Margies Cove Trail

Mountain

× 2,230 ft.

MOUNTAINS

2,495 ft. ×

× 1,889 ft.

2,253 ft. ×

× 1,804 ft.

Brittlebush
Trail

The Hike

Starting from the Margies Cove West Trailhead, the trail follows a closed road and meanders up the broad, gently sloping valley. You'll pass an old windmill site in the first half mile. Gradually the mountains close in on either side. After about 3.1 miles, the trail starts following a gravelly wash as the old road veers away. Watch for rock cairns and BLM (federal Bureau of Land Management) trail markers along this section. The rugged peaks and canyon walls add to the wilderness atmosphere. Our hike ends where the Brittlebush Trail comes in from the right, about 5.2 miles from the trailhead.—Bruce Grubbs and Stewart Aitchison

OTHER TRAVELERS, OTHER TIMES

A segment of the 1850s Butterfield Stage Line runs along the southern boundary of the North Maricopa Mountains Wilderness. This stage was the first reliable, relatively fast method of transportation between the eastern United States and California. The stage carried people, mail, and freight over 2,700 miles in less than twenty-five days. In its three-year history, the stage boasted that it was late only three times.

Miles and Directions

0.0 Begin at Margies Cove West Trailhead.

0.5 Pass old windmill site.

3.1 Trail leaves old road.

5.2 Stop at Brittlebush Trail junction.

10.4 Return to trailhead the same way you came.

GREEN TIP

Carry a reusable water container that you fill at the tap.
Bottled water is expensive; lots of petroleum is used to make
the plastic bottles; and they're a disposal nightmare.

9 Cave Creek Trail

North of Phoenix, the low-lying, flat Valley of the Sun abruptly gives way to the foothills of the New River Mountains, a complex of mesas, canyons, Sonoran Desert peaks, and even some seasonal streams. This loop hike follows portions of Cave Creek, one such creek within the southern portion of the New River Mountains in the Tonto National Forest.

Start: About 12 miles north of Carefree
Distance: 10.0-mile loop
Approximate hiking time: 6 hours
Elevation change: 1,040 feet
Difficulty: Moderate due to distance and elevation change
Seasons: Fall through spring
Trail surface: Dirt and rocks
Water: Seasonal in Cave Creek
Other trail users: Mountain bikes and horses

Land status: Tonto National Forest
Nearest town: Carefree
Fees and permits: None
Maps: USGS New River Mesa and Humboldt Mountain; Trail Illustrated Superstition and Four Peaks Wildernesses; USFS Tonto National Forest
Trail contact: Cave Creek Ranger District, Tonto National Forest

Finding the trailhead: From Carefree, drive east on Cave Creek Road until it becomes Forest Road 24. Drive 9 miles, past the Seven Springs and CCC campgrounds. Cross the creek twice to the Cave Creek Trailhead. GPS: N33 58.35'W111 51.99'

The Hike

Start on the Cave Creek Trail (Forest Trail 4), which follows the creek, crossing it a few times. After about 4 miles, turn left onto the Skunk Tank Trail. After another 5 miles, turn left onto Cottonwood Trail to return to the trailhead.

Along Cave Creek is a lovely riparian habitat featuring Fremont cottonwood and Arizona sycamore. This is a great birding area, especially in late spring and early summer.

Just inside the national forest boundary is a 0.5-mile side trip to Sears-Kay Ruin, the remains of a thousand-year-old Hohokam settlement. A self-guided tour includes signs explaining the site.—Stewart Aitchison

Miles and Directions

0.0 Begin at Cave Creek Trailhead.

4.0 Junction Skunk Tank Trail; turn left.

6.8 Reach high point of trail.

9.0 Junction with Cottonwood Trail; turn left.

10.0 Return to Cave Creek Trailhead.

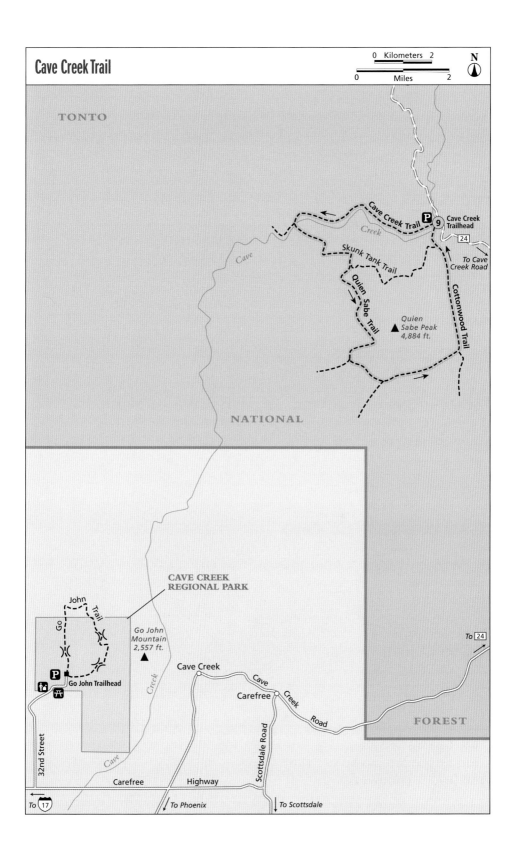

Cave Creek Trail

0   Kilometers   2

0   Miles   2

N

TONTO

Cave Creek Trail

P

9

Cave Creek
Trailhead

24

Creek

Cave

To Cave
Creek Road

Skunk Tank Trail

Quien Sabe Trail

Cottonwood Trail

Quien
Sabe Peak
4,884 ft.

NATIONAL

CAVE CREEK
REGIONAL PARK

Go John Trail

Go John
Mountain
2,557 ft.

To 24

P

Go John Trailhead

Creek

Cave Creek

Carefree

Cave

Creek

Road

FOREST

32nd Street

Cave

Scottsdale Road

Carefree   Highway

To 17

To Phoenix

To Scottsdale

Mazatzal Mountains

The Mazatzal Mountains encompass a wild variety of terrain—from desert plains to pine-forested mountains to rocky peaks—but deep, rugged canyons are the dominating feature of the landscape. From the Verde River on the west, the terrain rises eastward, at first gradually, then more abruptly as the quartzite backbone of the range is exposed. As the terrain rises, the low desert cactus and shrubs give way to high desert grasses and diminutive pinyon pine and juniper trees. Finally the range culminates in the 7,000-foot crest; several peaks reach nearly 8,000 feet. Outcrops of Precambrian Mazatzal quartzite, Maverick shale, and other rocks are often twisted and warped by the titanic forces that created these mountains back when the Rocky Mountains also were forming. Vegetation here is a mix of chaparral brush and ponderosa pine. There's even some Douglas fir, white fir, and quaking aspen mixed in on the cooler, north-facing slopes. The eastern slopes are quite abrupt, falling rapidly, sometimes in spectacular cliffs, to the desert valley of the Tonto Basin. The northern portion of the range is protected in the Mazatzal Wilderness, and the southernmost portion is accessible from several trailheads along Highway 87 in the Slate Creek Divide region.

◀ *You'll find awesome scenery as you look north along the Mazatzal Mountains from the Mazatzal Divide Trail near Mount Peeley.*

10 Marion Spring

This good day hike in the southeast corner of the Mazatzal Wilderness can be combined with the Squaw Flat hike to make a much longer day hike or overnight backpack trip. The trail starts from the Cross F Trailhead, one of the few Mazatzal Mountains trailheads that can be reached from a paved road.

Start: About 50 miles north of Mesa
Distance: 7.0 miles out and back
Approximate hiking time: 4-5 hours
Elevation change: 1,280 feet
Difficulty: Moderate due to distance and elevation change
Trail surface: Dirt and rocks
Water: Seasonally at Marion Spring
Seasons: Fall through spring
Other trail users: Horses

Land status: Mazatzal Wilderness, Tonto National Forest
Nearest town: Mesa
Fees and permits: Group size limited to 15; stay limit 14 days.
Maps: USGS Reno Pass and Lion Mountain; Trails Illustrated Mazatzal and Pine Mountain Wildernesses; USFS Mazatzal Wilderness, USFS Tonto National Forest
Trail contact: Mesa Ranger District, Tonto National Forest

Finding the trailhead: From Mesa, drive about 53 miles north on Highway 87 to the Mount Ord/Sycamore Creek exit; turn left and drive 3.4 miles to the end of the road and the Cross F Trailhead. A powerline crosses the road just before the trailhead. GPS: N33 54.46' W111 29.05'

The Hike

The Squaw Flat Trail starts on the west side of the highway and can be difficult to locate. It crosses under the power line, then heads west up an unnamed tributary of Sycamore Creek. It follows this tributary then meets the Arizona Trail; turn right (north). The trail turns northwest and climbs through a low saddle to meet an old jeep trail, which it follows to the northwest along a ridge. At the point where the Squaw Flat Trail turns northeast and starts to traverse the slopes south of Potato Patch, turn left and hike the short spur northwest to Marion Spring, our goal for this hike. You're on the south slopes of Saddle Mountain, visible to the north. To the south, you can see much of the rugged country west of Sycamore Creek.

Miles and Directions

0.0 Cross F Trailhead.
0.5 Turn right on the Arizona Trail.
2.6 Begin following old jeep trail.
3.2 Marion Spring junction; turn left.
3.5 Arrive at Marion Spring.

Marion Spring

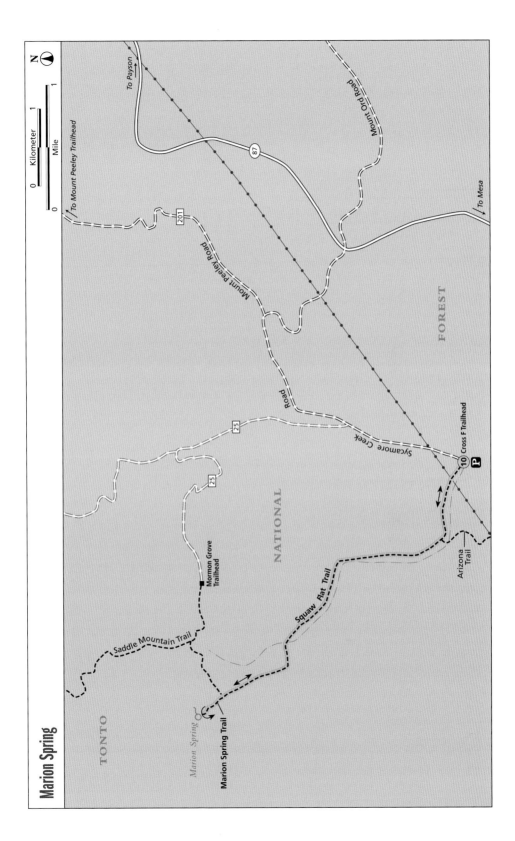

N

0   Kilometer   1
0   Mile   1

To Payson

To Mount Peeley Trailhead

87

Mount Ord Road

201

Mount Peeley Road

To Mesa

Road

25

25

FOREST

Sycamore Creek

Cross F Trailhead

10

P

NATIONAL

Mormon Grove
Trailhead

Arizona
Trail

Saddle Mountain Trail

Squaw Flat Trail

TONTO

Marion Spring

Marion Spring Trail

Clearing storm clouds scoot over Saddle Mountain in the southern Mazatzal Mountains.

7.0 Retrace your steps to trailhead.

Option

From the Marion Spring turnoff, you could continue 0.4 mile to the end of the Squaw Flat Trail at the Saddle Mountain Trail. By turning left, you can hike to Squaw Flat. (See the Squaw Flat hike description for more information.)

THIS WAY TO WATER

Arizona has quite a few "Sycamore Creeks," and when you see the namesake tree, you'll understand why. The Arizona sycamore is a massive, spreading, streamside tree with mottled greenish and brownish bark. Its large leaves usually have five points and resemble a maple's, while the seeds are found in fuzzy "buttonballs" that swing from slender stems. Arizona sycamore is a water-loving tree that grows along drainages, and its presence means that water is not far below the surface. If you're in need of water, look carefully as you hike along the streambed, because there are likely to be surface pools somewhere.

11 Squaw Flat

Less-visited country is the main attraction of this hike in the southern Mazatzal Wilderness. You'll also hike through stands of Arizona cypress, an uncommon tree that grows mainly in the mountains of central Arizona. Arizona cypress is easy to spot—the small, slender tree commonly grows to about 30 feet and features reddish, curling bark. A seasonal spring and views of much of the southwestern portion of the wilderness top off the hike.

Start: About 53 miles north of Mesa

Distance: 8.2 miles out and back

Approximate hiking time: 5 hours

Elevation change: 630 feet

Difficulty: Moderate due to distance and elevation change

Trail surface: Dirt and rocks

Water: Seasonal at Squaw Flat Spring

Seasons: Fall through spring

Other trail users: Horses

Land status: Mazatzal Wilderness, Tonto National Forest.

Nearest town: Mesa

Fees and permits: Group size limited to 15; stay limit 14 days.

Maps: USGS Reno Pass and Lion Mountain; Trails Illustrated Mazatzal and Pine Mountain Wildernesses; USFS Mazatzal Wilderness, USFS Tonto National Forest

Trail contact: Mesa Ranger District, Tonto National Forest.

Finding the trailhead: From Mesa, drive about 53 miles north on Highway 87, then turn off at the Mount Ord exit. Turn left onto Sycamore Creek Road, drive 2.4 miles, and then turn right onto Forest Road 25. Continue 3.3 miles to the end of the road at the Mormon Grove Trailhead. GPS: N33 56.33' W111 30.43'

The Hike

Start the hike on the Saddle Mountain Trail, an old mining road that climbs the ridge west of the trailhead, then passes through a saddle and swings north to another saddle, meeting the junction with the Little Saddle Trail. Stay right on the Saddle Mountain Trail as it contours north along the east slopes of a ridge, which are covered with dense chaparral brush. You'll have some good views into the West Fork of Sycamore Creek, to the east. Finally, the trail passes through another saddle on the southeast slopes of Saddle Mountain. The gently sloping desert grassland you see to the west is known as Potato Patch. Now follow the trail around the east side of Saddle Mountain.

Here the Cornucopia Trail goes right; stay left on the Saddle Mountain Trail and follow it north into McFarland Canyon. The head of McFarland Canyon is thickly forested with Arizona cypress, which is fairly common in the northern Mazatzal Mountains. At this point the little-used Thicket Spring Trail branches right, but stay left on Saddle Mountain Trail past Squaw Flat Spring, which is in the bed of McFarland Canyon. Just beyond the spring, turn right onto the Sheep Creek Trail, which

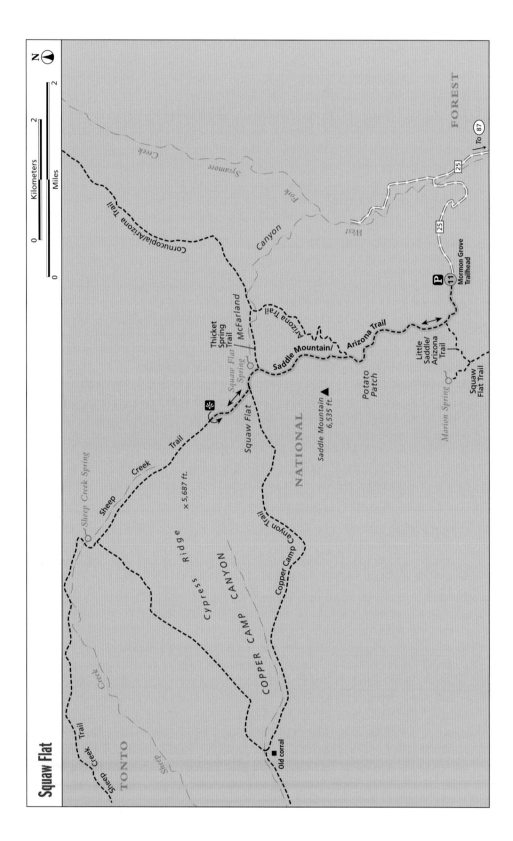

Squaw Flat

N

Kilometers
0   2

Miles
0   2

FOREST

To 87

25

25

Mormon Grove
Trailhead

P 11

Little
Saddle/
Arizona
Trail

Arizona Trail

Marion Spring

Squaw
Flat Trail

West

Fork

Sycamore

Creek

Canyon

Cornucopia/Arizona Trail

Thicket
Spring
Trail

McFarland

Arizona Trail

Squaw Flat Spring

Squaw Flat

Saddle Mountain/

Saddle Mountain
6,535 ft.

Potato
Patch

NATIONAL

Sheep Creek Spring

Sheep   Creek   Trail

Cypress   Ridge

×5,687 ft.

Copper Camp Canyon Trail

COPPER CAMP CANYON

Old corral

Sheep   Creek   Trail

Sheep   Creek

TONTO

climbs out of the bed, then heads northwest across Squaw Flat, the hilly basin at the head of McFarland Canyon. The destination for our hike is the rim at the head of Sheep Creek. This vantage point offers sweeping views of the southern portion of the Mazatzal Wilderness. The saddle-shaped peak to the south is appropriately named Saddle Mountain. The bulk of Sheep Mountain looms to the northeast, and the steep canyons that form the head of Sheep Creek dominate the view to the north and northwest.

Miles and Directions

0.0 Mormon Grove Trailhead.

0.5 Trail passes junction with Little Saddle Trail.

2.0 Cornucopia Trail junction; stay left.

3.2 Thicket Spring Trail (Arizona Trail) junction; stay left.

3.5 Sheep Creek Trail junction; turn right.

4.1 Arrive at viewpoint.

8.2 Return to trailhead the way you came.

Stormy weather over the Mazatzal Mountains is a good reminder to check the weather forecast before your hike.

12 Copper Camp Canyon

Another hike into the seldom-visited southern end of the Mazatzal Wilderness, this trek is for backpackers who want a challenging trail and cross-country hike into beautiful and remote country less than 50 airline miles from downtown Phoenix. There are two seasonal springs, and great views reward you after the steep climb up from Sheep Creek.

Start: About 53 miles north of Mesa
Distance: 16.9-mile loop
Approximate hiking time: 11 hours or 2 days
Elevation change: 5,530 feet
Difficulty: Strenuous due to distance and elevation change
Trail surface: Dirt and rocks
Water: Seasonal at Squaw Flat Spring and Sheep Creek Seep
Seasons: Fall through spring
Other trail users: Horses

Land status: Mazatzal Wilderness, Tonto National Forest
Nearest town: Mesa
Fees and permits: Group size limited to 15; stay limit 14 days.
Maps: USGS Reno Pass and Lion Mountain; Trails Illustrated Mazatzal and Pine Mountain Wildernesses; USFS Mazatzal Wilderness, USFS Tonto National Forest
Trail contact: Mesa Ranger District, Tonto National Forest

Finding the trailhead: From Mesa, drive about 53 miles north on Highway 87, then turn off at the Mount Ord exit. Turn left onto the Sycamore Creek Road, drive 2.4 miles, and then turn right onto Forest Road 25. Continue 3.3 miles to the end of the road at the Mormon Grove Trailhead. GPS: N33 56.33' W111 30.43'

Special considerations: Some of the trails on this hike get very little use and can be difficult to find. You should have both the wilderness map and the USGS maps and be skilled in map reading and cross-country travel before attempting this hike.

The Hike

Start the hike on the Saddle Mountain Trail, which climbs the ridge west of the trailhead, then passes through two saddles, passing the junction with the Little Saddle Trail. The trail contours north along the east slopes of a ridge, and then passes through another saddle on the southeast slopes of Saddle Mountain. Follow the trail around the east side of Saddle Mountain.

When the Cornucopia Trail (Arizona Trail) goes right, stay left on the Saddle Mountain Trail and follow it north into McFarland Canyon. Stay left at the junction with the Thicket Spring Trail. There should be seasonal water at Squaw Flat Spring, which is in the bed of McFarland Canyon. Just west of Squaw Flat Spring, turn left onto the Copper Camp Trail at the junction with the Sheep Creek Trail, which will be our return on the loop portion of the hike.

Agave grows in the southern Mazatzal Mountains.

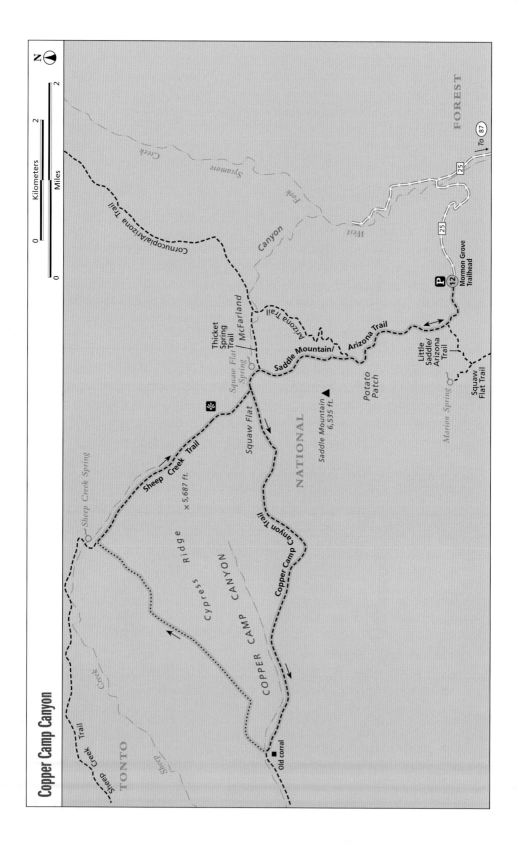

Copper Camp Canyon

N

Kilometers
0   2

Miles
0   2

TONTO

NATIONAL

FOREST

Sheep Creek Trail

Sheep Creek

Sheep Creek Spring

Cypress Ridge

x 5,687 ft.

Sheep Creek Trail

Cornucopia/Arizona Trail

Sycamore Creek

West Fork

Canyon

Squaw Flat Trail

Thicket Spring Trail

Squaw Flat Spring

McFarland

Arizona Trail

Saddle Mountain/

Squaw Flat

Copper Camp Canyon Trail

COPPER CAMP CANYON

Old corral

Saddle Mountain
6,535 ft.

Potato Patch

Arizona Trail

Little Saddle/
Arizona Trail

Marion Spring

Squaw Flat Trail

25

P   12
Mormon Grove
Trailhead

25

To 87

The Copper Camp Trail continues a gradual climb west to the head of McFarland Canyon, then heads out onto a brushy ridge. This trail gets very little use and can be hard to find. It is shown on the wilderness and Trails Illustrated maps. Soon the trail descends steeply down a ridge to the southwest. It turns northwest shortly after, then west, working its way toward Copper Camp Creek through a complex of ridges and small canyons. After skirting a low ridge on the south, it drops into Copper Camp Creek and stays there. Watch for an old corral about 0.6 mile downstream from the point where the trail meets the bed. This is the lowest point of the hike and the start of the cross-country segment.

Leave the trail here and follow an old route northeast onto Cypress Ridge. Very few traces of trail remain, and the route is essentially cross-country. This old trail is shown on the wilderness map as an informal trail but not on the USGS or Trails Illustrated maps. Generally work your way east-northeast, staying on the ridge just north of Copper Camp Creek, toward the crest of Cypress Ridge, clearly visible above. You should reach the crest at a point about 0.3 mile west of Point 5,126 on the USGS Lion Mountain topo. After the steep climb, the plateau-like north slope of Cypress Ridge is a welcome sight. Now work your way northeast toward Sheep Creek Seep, which is shown correctly on the Lion Mountain map but not on the wilderness map. Much of the plateau is open grassland, though there are some large areas of dense chaparral brush to avoid. The route drops into Sheep Creek at another old corral just northwest of Sheep Creek Seep and meets the Sheep Creek Trail. There is seasonal water in Sheep Creek and at the seep.

Turn right onto the Sheep Creek Trail, little-used but easy to track, and follow it southeast up Sheep Creek. The grade is moderate for a while, but then steepens as the trail leaves the creek and climbs to the rim of Squaw Flat. Your reward for all the hard work is tremendous views of much of the country you've just hiked. Continue southeast down the gently sloping Squaw Flat into McFarland Canyon, then turn left onto the Saddle Mountain Trail to complete the loop. Remain on the Saddle Mountain Trail to return to the Mormon Grove Trailhead.

Miles and Directions

0.0 Begin at Mormon Grove Trailhead.

0.5 Trail passes junction with Little Saddle Trail.

2.0 Cornucopia Trail junction; stay left.

3.2 Thicket Spring Trail junction; stay left.

3.5 Copper Camp Trail junction; turn left.

7.8 Old corral; leave the trail and hike northeast toward Cypress Ridge.

9.1 Arrive at Cypress Ridge.

10.9 Meet the Sheep Creek Trail; turn right.

12.8 End climb to rim of Squaw Flat.

13.4 Copper Camp Trail junction; turn right.

16.9 Return to Mormon Grove Trailhead.

13 Mazatzal Divide Trail

The Mazatzal Divide Trail is the premier trail in the Mazatzal Wilderness and runs nearly the entire length of the northern half of the Mazatzal Mountains, staying on or near the crest of this 6,000- to nearly 8,000-foot range. The Arizona Trail follows the Mazatzal Divide Trail for most of its Mazatzal Mountains passage. This hike explores the southern end of the Mazatzal Divide Trail, which alternates cool, shady stretches of ponderosa pine forest with 100-mile views.

Start: About 60 miles north of Mesa

Distance: 15.6 miles out and back

Approximate hiking time:
12 hours or 2 days

Elevation change: 2,360 feet

Difficulty: Strenuous due to distance and elevation change

Seasons: Fall through spring

Trail surface: Dirt and rocks

Water: Seasonally at Fisher Spring, Bear Spring, Windsor Spring, Brody Seep, Chilson Spring, Horse Camp Seep, and Hopi Spring

Other trail users: Horses

Land status: Mazatzal Wilderness, Tonto National Forest

Nearest town: Mesa

Fees and permits: Group size limited to 15; stay limit 14 days.

Maps: USGS Mazatzal Peak, North Peak, and Cypress Butte; Trails Illustrated Mazatzal and Pine Mountain Wildernesses; USFS Mazatzal Wilderness, USFS Tonto National Forest

Trail contacts: Mesa, Tonto Basin, and Payson Ranger Districts, Tonto National Forest

Finding the trailhead: From Mesa, drive about 53 miles north on Highway 87, then turn left at the Mount Ord/Sycamore Creek exit. After 1.2 miles, turn right onto Forest Road 201 and follow this graded dirt road about 8.7 miles north and west to its end at the Mount Peeley Trailhead. GPS: N34 0.29' W111 28.78'

Special considerations: Because the Mazatzal Divide Trail stays high on ridges most of the way, water can be a problem. None of the springs on or near the trail are reliable. It's best to do this hike in the spring after snowmelt or in the fall after a wet summer. Don't depend on any single water source. The trail was rerouted in the 1970s and is not always shown correctly on the USGS maps.

The Hike

Start on the Cornucopia Trail, an old mining road, and follow the trail as it winds west along the ridge dividing the Deer Creek and Sycamore Creek drainages, then turns south along the east slopes of Mount Peeley, where the Mazatzal Divide Trail forks right and climbs west up a brushy slope. After a couple of switchbacks, the trail swings around the north side of Mount Peeley and levels off. As it continues to contour west

Fisher Spring is one of the few springs located near the Mazatzal Divide Trail.

Mazatzal Divide Trail

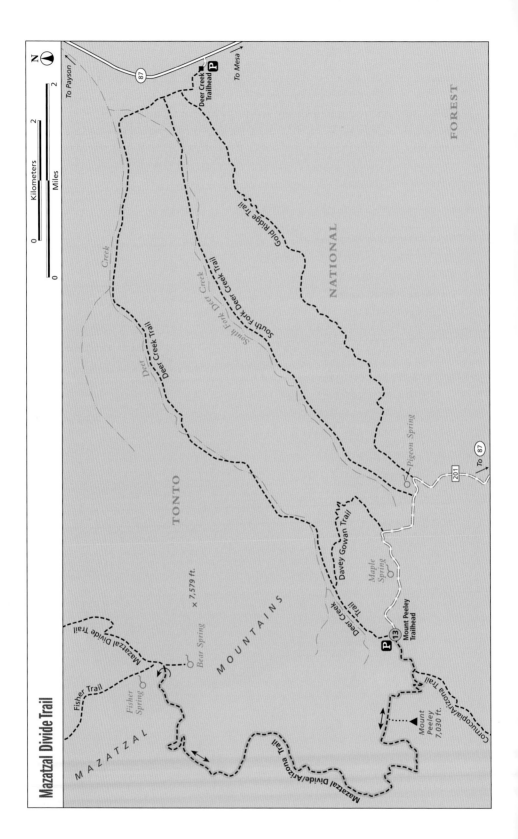

N

To Payson

To Mesa

87

Deer Creek Trailhead

P

Gold Ridge Trail

South Fork Deer Creek Trail

South Fork Deer Creek

Deer Creek

Deer Creek Trail

Creek

TONTO

NATIONAL

FOREST

Pigeon Spring

201

To 87

Davey Gowan Trail

Maple Spring

× 7,579 ft.

Bear Spring

MOUNTAINS

Deer Creek Trail

Mount Peeley Trailhead

P 13

Fisher Spring

Fisher Trail

Mazatzal Divide Trail

MAZATZAL

Cornucopia/Arizona Trail

Mazatzal Divide/Arizona Trail

Mount Peeley 7,030 ft.

Kilometers

Miles

0   2

0   2

around the head of one of the many forks of Deer Creek, it enters a fine stand of ponderosa pine. Finally, the trail contours into a saddle on the crest of the Mazatzal Mountains, then heads north along the crest. After a fairly level section, the Mazatzal Divide Trail starts to climb gradually and turns eastward. The trail reaches its highest point just south of Peak 7,221, then descends east to Fisher Saddle, which is the goal for the hike. Bear Spring is located about 0.3 mile south on a spur trail, and Fisher Spring about the same distance north on the Fisher Trail, but 450 feet lower than the saddle.

Miles and Directions

0.0 Start at Mount Peeley Trailhead.

0.5 Mazatzal Divide Trail junction; turn right.

6.4 Trail reaches high point.

7.8 Arrive at Fisher Saddle.

15.6 Return to trailhead.

Option

From the point where the trail first enters the pine forest on the north slopes of Mount Peeley, you can easily hike cross-country about 0.5 mile to the summit of Mount Peeley. It's about 500 feet of climbing, but the going is easy and the views of the southern portion of the wilderness from the rounded, rocky summit of this 7,030-foot peak are worth it.

14 Deer Creek

This loop hike traverses several deep canyons in the eastern portion of the Mazatzal Wilderness and has several options for exploring the forks of Deer Creek. The return portion of the loop descends a spectacular ridge, taking you from pine and fir forest on the crest of the Mazatzal Mountains to desert grasslands and treating you to yet more stunning views along the way.

Start: About 63 miles north of Mesa
Distance: 15.8-mile loop backpack or long day hike
Approximate hiking time: 10 hours or 2 days
Elevation change: 3,800 feet
Difficulty: Strenuous due to distance and elevation change
Seasons: Fall through spring
Trail surface: Dirt and rocks
Water: Seasonal in Deer Creek and at Maple and Pigeon Springs
Other trail users: Horses

Land status: Mazatzal Wilderness, Tonto National Forest
Nearest town: Mesa
Fees and permits: Group size limited to 15; stay limit 14 days.
Maps: USGS Mazatzal Peak; Trails Illustrated Mazatzal and Pine Mountain Wildernesses; USFS Mazatzal Wilderness, USFS Tonto National Forest
Trail contact: Tonto Basin Ranger District, Tonto National Forest

Finding the trailhead: From Mesa, drive about 63 miles north on Highway 87. Turn left into the Deer Creek Trailhead, just south of the junction with Highway 188. GPS: N34 2.18' W111 22.16'

The Hike

From the trailhead, start northwest on the Deer Creek Trail (Forest Trail 45) as it climbs onto a low ridge. The Gold Ridge Trail, which will be our return from the loop portion of the hike, branches left. Soon the South Fork Trail also branches left; stay right on the Deer Creek Trail at both junctions. The Deer Creek Trail crosses the South Fork of Deer Creek, then turns west into Deer Creek just upstream of a ranch located on private land. Now the trail follows the creek west toward the mountains. Although the stream flow is seasonal, depending on recent rain and snow, the canyon bottom is still shaded by Arizona sycamore and other streamside trees. When Deer Creek starts a turn southwest, Bars Canyon joins from the right. As you continue upstream along Deer Creek, the trail becomes fainter but always stays near the bottom of the canyon. The appearance of the first ponderosa pine along the north-facing slopes signals that you're reaching the head of the canyon. After an unnamed tributary canyon comes in from the northwest, Deer Creek swings to the south briefly before resuming its southwesterly direction. You'll hike through a brushy meadow, then meet the Davey Gowan Trail (Forest Trail 48).

Deer Creek

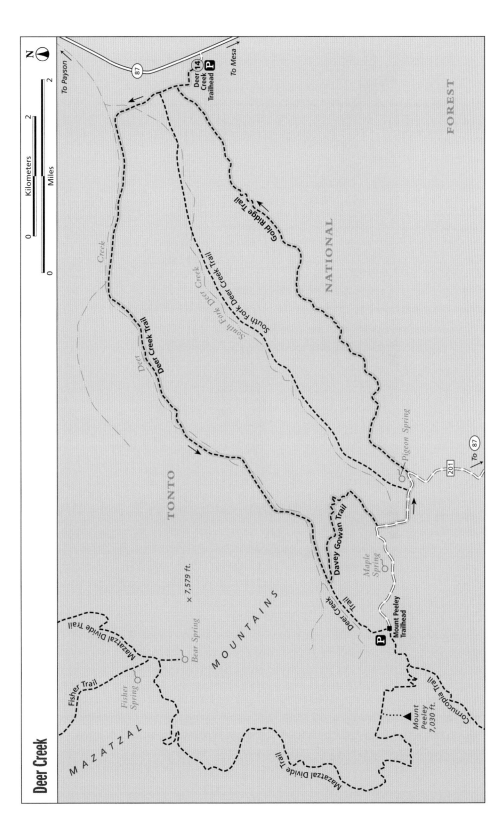

N

To Payson

87

Deer (14) Creek Trailhead **P**

To Mesa

Kilometers

0   2

Miles

0   2

Creek

Deer Creek Trail

Deer Creek

South Fork Deer Creek

South Fork Deer Creek Trail

Gold Ridge Trail

TONTO

x 7,579 ft.

NATIONAL

FOREST

Pigeon Spring

201

To **87**

Davey Gowan Trail

Maple Spring

Deer Creek Trail

Mount Peeley Trailhead

P

Bear Spring

Mazatzal Divide Trail

Fisher Trail

Fisher Spring

MAZATZAL

MOUNTAINS

Mount Peeley 7,030 ft.

Mazatzal Divide Trail

Cornucopia Trail

Mountain lions are rarely encountered by hikers. This one is at the Arizona Sonora Desert Museum.

Turn left here and follow the Davey Gowan Trail as it climbs east out of the canyon, then swings south onto a ridge and climbs to meet the Mount Peeley Road (Forest Road 201). Turn left onto the road and hike east past the South Fork Trailhead to a spur road branching left and downhill. Follow this road northeast to a road closure and the start of the Gold Ridge Trail (Forest Trail 47). The trail, an old jeep road, drops off the northwest side of the ridge, then swings east to follow the general ridge system. You'll leave the pine forest behind as the trail descends onto lower, drier slopes. Watch for the point where the old jeep road veers north and the Gold Ridge Trail becomes a foot trail, heading east for a short distance before turning northeast

WATCH FOR BIG CATS

Look for mountain lion tracks along the dusty sections of the trail, especially early in the morning. The prints are larger than any dog's, and the lack of claw marks confirms that the track was made by a large cat. Bobcat tracks are much smaller. The remote canyons of the Mazatzal Mountains are favored terrain for these large cats. Mountain lions, also known as cougars, require large amounts of territory remote from human influence. You may see their tracks, but you'll be very lucky to see the actual animal. Bobcats are more common, though still rare. They occasionally jump in front of a vehicle on a dirt road and run for a few dozen yards before vanishing into the underbrush. In the backcountry, you'll be lucky to have a fleeting glimpse. Bobcats resemble an oversize housecat, except for their short "bobbed" tail.

again. It descends a ridge that gives you great views to the northeast, then finally emerges onto gentler slopes covered with high desert grasses. Continue to the Deer Creek Trail and turn right to return to the Deer Creek Trailhead.

Miles and Directions

0.0 Start at Deer Creek Trailhead.

0.4 Gold Ridge Trail junction; stay right.

0.6 South Fork Trail junction; stay right.

1.2 The trail turns west up Deer Creek.

7.4 Davey Gowan Trail junction; turn left.

9.0 Mount Peeley Road; turn left.

9.7 Pass the South Fork Trailhead; stay right on Mount Peeley Road.

9.9 Road to the Gold Ridge Trail; turn left.

10.4 Road closure; begin descent.

15.4 Deer Creek Trail junction; turn right.

15.8 Deer Creek Trailhead.

Options

Option 1. Instead of leaving Deer Creek on the Davey Gowan Trail, stay right and follow the Deer Creek Trail southwest as it climbs through dense pine-fir forest to the Mount Peeley Trailhead. Turn left and walk the Mount Peeley Road 1.4 miles to the Davey Gowan Trail junction (Forest Trail 48), then continue 0.9 mile east to the Gold Ridge Trail. This option gets you into the head of Deer Creek, though it involves a little more road walking. It adds 0.7 mile and less than an hour to the loop.

Option 2. From Mount Peeley Road, return via the South Fork Trail (Forest Trail 46). This little-used trail leaves the road 0.7 mile east of the Davey Gowan Trail before dropping into the South Fork of Deer Creek. (See South Fork of Deer Creek for details.) This option is 0.2 mile shorter.

15 South Fork of Deer Creek

An alternative to hiking the more-popular main fork of Deer Creek is to take the south fork, which provides easy access into a seldom-visited area of the Mazatzal Wilderness. You'll start in the desert grasslands of Tonto Basin and end up in ponderosa pine–Douglas fir forest near the crest of the Mazatzal Mountains.

Start: About 63 miles north of Mesa

Distance: 11.8 miles out and back

Approximate hiking time: 7 hours or 2 days

Elevation change: 2,820 feet

Difficulty: Strenuous due to distance and elevation change

Seasons: Fall through spring

Trail surface: Dirt and rocks

Water: Seasonal along the South Fork of Deer Creek and at Pigeon Spring

Other trail users: Horses

Land status: Mazatzal Wilderness, Tonto National Forest

Nearest town: Mesa

Fees and permits: Group size limited to 15; stay limit 14 days.

Maps: USGS Mazatzal Peak; Trails Illustrated Mazatzal and Pine Mountain Wildernesses; USFS Mazatzal Wilderness, USFS Tonto National Forest

Trail contact: Tonto Basin Ranger District, Tonto National Forest

Finding the trailhead: From Mesa, drive about 63 miles north on Highway 87. Turn left into the Deer Creek Trailhead, just south of the junction with Highway 188. GPS: N34 2.18' W111 22.16'

The Hike

The trail starts in Sonoran Desert grassland and takes you through the chaparral brush and pinyon pine–juniper zone into lush pine-fir forest. Although the entire trail makes for a long day hike, you can hike just a portion of the trail and turn back when ready or do the trip as an overnight backpack. The South Fork is only a couple of miles shorter than the main fork of Deer Creek, and it heads into equally interesting country.

From the trailhead, start on the Deer Creek Trail (Forest Trail 45), hike past the Gold Ridge Trail (Forest Trail 47), then turn left onto the South Fork Trail (Forest Trail 46). The trail soon drops into the streambed. At first, the South Fork is fairly open, but within a mile the canyon deepens. Arizona sycamore, cottonwood, and other riparian (stream-loving) trees shade the trail as it follows the canyon southwest into the mountains. The creek itself may or may not be flowing, depending on how wet the weather has been. As you progress farther up the canyon, the trail becomes fainter. About 4.0 miles from the trailhead, the first ponderosa pines appear on north-facing slopes, though the opposite canyon wall is still covered with chaparral brush,

Watch for the ruin of an old stone cabin along the South Fork of Deer Creek.

South Fork of Deer Creek

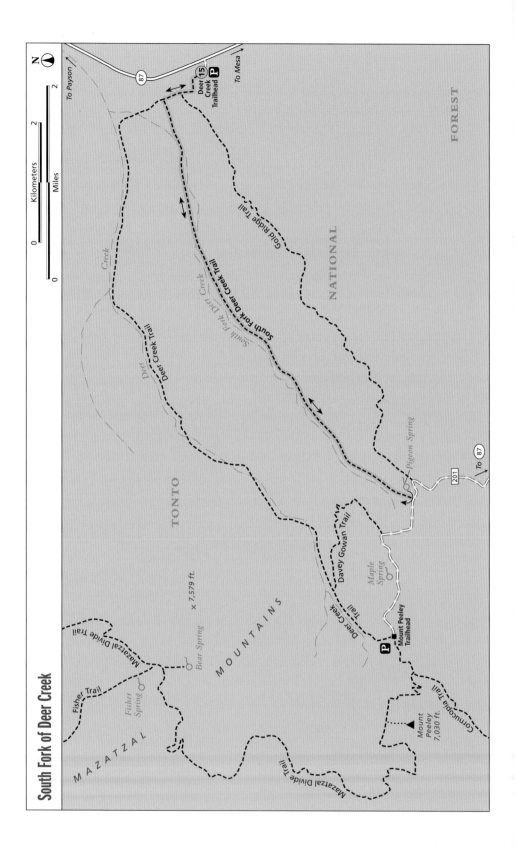

N

To Payson

87

Deer Creek Trailhead 15 P

To Mesa

Kilometers
Miles

Creek

Deer Creek Trail

Deer Creek

South Fork Deer Creek

South Fork Deer Creek Trail

Gold Ridge Trail

TONTO

NATIONAL

FOREST

× 7,579 ft.

Bear Spring

Mazatzal Divide Trail

Fisher Trail

Fisher Spring

MAZATZAL

M O U N T A I N S

Davey Gowan Trail

Maple Spring

Deer Creek Trail

Pigeon Spring

201

To 87

Mount Peeley Trailhead

P

Mount Peeley
7,030 ft.

Cornucopia Trail

Mazatzal Divide Trail

scattered juniper, and pinyon pine. Near the head of the canyon, the trail swings more to the south and climbs steeply. The last mile of the South Fork Trail passes through a fine stand of ponderosa pine and Douglas fir, then ends at Mount Peeley Road. Return to the trailhead the way you came.

Miles and Directions

0.0   Begin at Deer Creek Trailhead.

0.4   Pass Gold Ridge Trail junction.

0.6   South Fork Trail junction; turn left.

5.9   Mount Peeley Road.

11.8   Retrace your steps to trailhead.

Option

You could use the Gold Ridge or take the Davey Gowan and Deer Creek Trails to return to the Deer Creek Trailhead, making this into a loop hike. (See the Deer Creek hike description for information on these optional trails.)

LITTLE LIKELIHOOD OF BEARS

A few black bears are still found in the Mazatzal Mountains. Because they were hunted heavily for many years, the survivors are reclusive. You're more likely to see their tracks and their scat than the animal. Another sign of their presence is chewed-up trail signs.

Four Peaks

The Mazatzal Mountains rise abruptly north of the Salt River. The deep river gorge, now filled by Canyon Lake and Apache Lake reservoirs, divides the Superstition Mountains from the Mazatzal Mountains. The two ranges are completely different in character, which is surprising considering how few air miles separate them. The Mazatzal Mountains are one of a number of ranges that trend from north–northwest to south–southeast in central Arizona. The range is bounded by Tonto Basin on the east and the Verde River on the west. Sonoran Desert foothills covered with mesquite, saguaro and cholla cacti, and other distinct desert plants border the Verde River. The southern portion of the range culminates at Four Peaks, a group of four distinctive 7,000-foot summits easily visible from the Phoenix area on clear days. The terrain rises more gradually on the west side of the range and falls off steeply on the east. North of Four Peaks, the crest of the range dips somewhat, rises again at the summit of Mount Ord, then falls abruptly to Slate Creek Divide. As Highway 87 crosses from the west to the east side, it divides the range into north and south halves. The lowest slopes of the Four Peaks Wilderness are lower Sonoran Desert, the intermediate elevations are pinyon-juniper woodland, and the highest areas are covered with dense chaparral brush. The north-facing slopes along the highest peaks are covered with a mixed ponderosa pine–Gambel oak woodland.

Wildfires have repeatedly scorched the Four Peaks area. The largest of these burned the entire mountain from desert to summits in the summer of 1996, one of the driest fire seasons on record. Because of this, dead trees commonly fall across the trails in the Four Peaks Wilderness, and hikers should expect slow going at times. Despite all the fires, pockets of tall pines have survived, and smaller plants always grow back quickly. After a wet winter or summer rainy season, the open burned areas are a riot of wildflowers.

◀ *Indian paintbrush is found from low desert to pine forests and has a long flowering season.*

16 Camp Creek

This trail is north of the Four Peaks Wilderness and south of Slate Creek Divide, in the southern half of the Mazatzal Mountains. The hike starts amid granite boulders in classic Sonoran Desert terrain and climbs onto intermediate-elevation slopes higher in the mountains. As an option, you can hike through the ponderosa pine stands near the crest of the range and on to the far end of the trail at the Cline Trailhead.

Start: About 30 miles north of Mesa

Distance: 9.2 miles out and back

Approximate hiking time: 6 hours

Elevation change: 1,980 feet

Difficulty: Strenuous due to distance and elevation change

Seasons: Fall through spring

Trail surface: Dirt and rocks

Water: Seasonal in Camp Creek

Other trail users: Horses

Land status: Tonto National Forest

Nearest town: Mesa

Fees and permits: None

Maps: USGS Boulder Mountain; Trail Illustrated Superstition and Four Peaks Wildernesses; USFS Tonto National Forest

Trail contact: Mesa Ranger District, Tonto National Forest

Finding the trailhead: The Ballentine Trailhead is the easiest trailhead to reach in the Four Peaks area. From Highway 87 at Shea Boulevard, drive about 21 miles north to the signed trailhead on the right side of the highway. GPS: N33 45.77' W111 29.65'

The Hike

The Pine Creek Trail climbs east away from the highway for a short distance, then swings northeast onto the ridge north of Camp Creek. As the trail swings back to the east, it drops into Camp Creek itself, then follows the creek (which has seasonal water) generally east. Near the headwaters of Camp Creek, the trail crosses a flat and enters the mouth of Ballentine Canyon, the goal for this hike.

Miles and Directions

0.0 Begin at Ballentine Trailhead.

4.6 Enter Ballentine Canyon.

9.2 Retrace your steps to trailhead.

Option

The Pine Creek Trail can be followed farther up Ballentine Canyon to its end at the Cline Trailhead, a distance of 10.2 miles from the Ballentine Trailhead. As the Pine Creek Trail nears the crest of the Mazatzal Mountains, the canyon and trail veer south and the trail tops out at a saddle just east of Pine Mountain, at 8.2 miles. Now the trail drops steeply into the headwaters of Picadilla Creek, passing Mountain Spring, and ends at the Cline Trailhead. GPS: N33 45.87' W111 29.60'

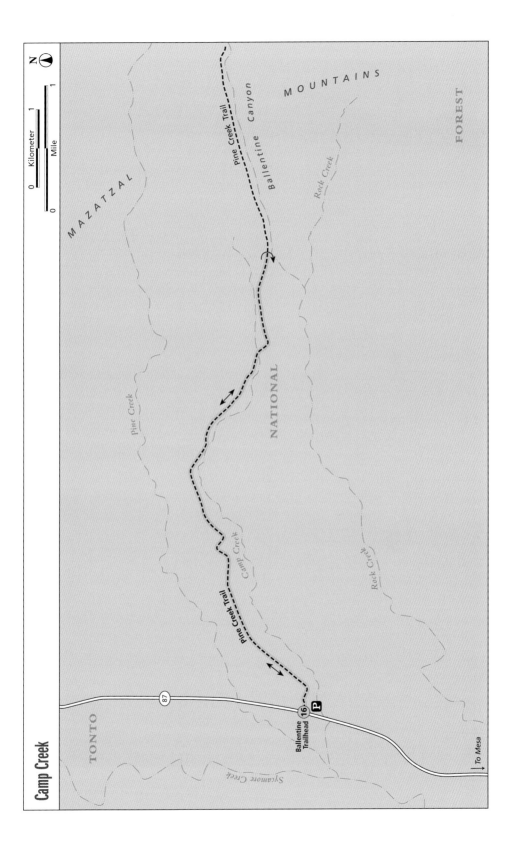

Camp Creek

TONTO

MAZATZAL

MOUNTAINS

NATIONAL

FOREST

Pine Creek Trail

Ballentine Canyon

Pine Creek

Camp Creek

Pine Creek Trail

Sycamore Creek

Rock Creek

Rock Creek

87

16 Ballentine
Trailhead

P

To Mesa

N

0   Kilometer   1

0   1   Mile

A storm clears over the Sonoran Desert near the lower section of the Camp Creek Trail.

17 Browns Peak

Browns Peak is the highest, northernmost summit of Four Peaks, the prominent group of peaks at the southern end of the Mazatzal Mountains and within Four Peaks Wilderness. Most of the hike is on trail, but the ascent of the peak requires cross-country travel, and the summit involves a short rock scramble. Since Four Peaks is visible from so many places in the Phoenix area, you would expect the views from this 7,657-foot summit to be panoramic, and you won't be disappointed. This is the highest hike in this book.

Start: About 30 miles northeast of Mesa
Distance: 4.0 miles out and back
Approximate hiking time: 3-4 hours
Elevation change: 2,030 feet
Difficulty: Strenuous due to distance and elevation change
Seasons: Spring through fall
Trail surface: Dirt and rocks
Water: None
Other trail users: Horses on the trail portion of the hike

Land status: Four Peaks Wilderness, Tonto National Forest
Nearest town: Mesa
Fees and permits: Group size limited to 15; stay limit 14 days.
Maps: USGS Four Peaks; Trail Illustrated Superstition and Four Peaks Wildernesses; USFS Tonto National Forest
Trail contact: Mesa Ranger District, Tonto National Forest

Finding the trailhead: From Mesa, drive northeast on Highway 87. At Shea Boulevard, note your mileage, and continue 14 miles to Forest Road 143. Turn right onto this maintained dirt road, which becomes unmaintained and much rougher after 6.7 miles. When you are 18.3 miles from the highway, turn right onto Forest Road 648 and continue 1.0 mile south to the Lone Pine Saddle Trailhead at the end of the road. GPS: N33 42.331'W111 20.274'

The Hike

Start on the Browns Trail, which climbs south from the trailhead through a fine stand of ponderosa pine and Gambel oak. Luckily, this stand was nearly untouched by the Lone Fire of 1996. The trail now swings southwest, then turns southeast, back toward the main ridge. Here it enters an area where the Lone Fire destroyed nearly all the trees. Be alert for falling trees, which can topple at any time. Windy and wet weather is especially hazardous. As consolation, the distant view is better without the forest.

After crossing the main ridge, the trail works its way up the northeast slopes with an occasional switchback. After crossing the Amethyst Trail, the trail ends at Browns Saddle. Leave the trail here and continue south, cross-country, up the ridge toward Browns Peak. Though the craggy peak looks impressive, it's actually easy to climb, and you'll need your hands in only a few places. Note the prominent ravine that splits the

Browns Peak is the left-most of the four rocky summits that make up Four Peaks.

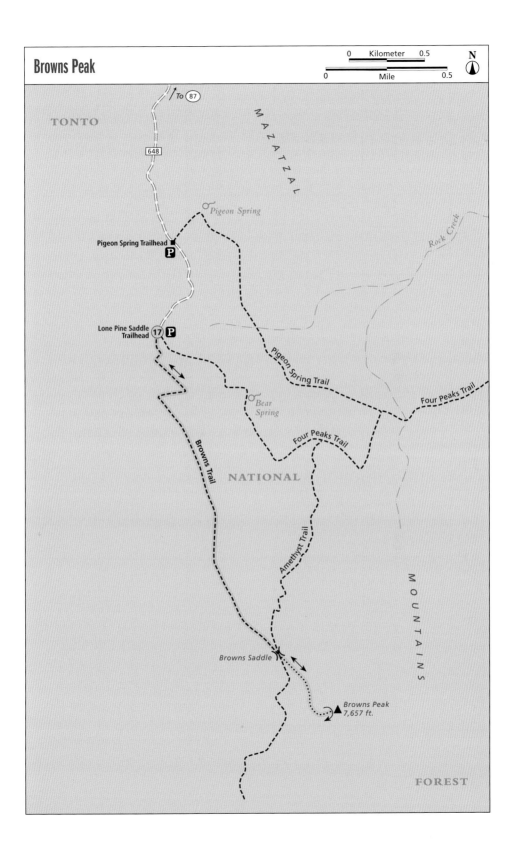

Browns Peak

0   Kilometer   0.5

0   Mile   0.5

N

TONTO

MAZATZAL

To 87

648

Pigeon Spring

Pigeon Spring Trailhead   P

Rock Creek

Lone Pine Saddle
Trailhead   17   P

Pigeon Spring Trail

Four Peaks Trail

Bear
Spring

Browns Trail

Four Peaks Trail

NATIONAL

Amethyst Trail

MOUNTAINS

Browns Saddle

Browns Peak
7,657 ft.

FOREST

north face of the peak. This is your goal, but you won't be able to see it when you get closer.

Although you can reach the summit by several different routes, the following route is one of the easiest. When you reach the first rock outcrops, turn right and work your way into the main gully that drains the ravine mentioned above. If you stay high, right at the base of the rock, you'll avoid the worst of the brush. Then head directly up the ravine. There's one spot in the ravine where you'll need your hands. The ravine tops out on the west shoulder of the peak, and it's then a short scramble to the left (east) to reach the summit.

From this lofty vantage point, you can see much of the country covered by this guide. Though the bulk of the other three peaks blocks some of the view to the south, you can still see much of the Superstition Mountains. To the west lies the Valley of the Sun, containing Phoenix and its sister cities. The desert plain is dotted with low mountain ranges that seem to recede into the distance. On a clear day you can see the McDowell Mountains and, far to the west, the Harquahala Mountains. To the northwest, the bulk of the Bradshaw Mountains looms above the lower-elevation New River Mountains. The Mazatzal Mountains run north-northwest from your perch—the rounded summit of Mount Ord, crowned with radio towers and a fire lookout, is clearly visible. The rugged peaks of the Mazatzal Wilderness form the backdrop for Mount Ord. North and eastward, the clean line of the Mogollon Rim slices across the horizon near Payson, and to the east the wide bulk of the Sierra Ancha dominates the skyline. To the southeast, you can see Pinal Peak, rising above the town of Globe.

Miles and Directions

0.0   Begin at Lone Pine Saddle Trailhead.

1.5   Junction with Amethyst Trail; continue straight through Browns Saddle and leave trail.

2.0   Reach Browns Peak.

4.0   Follow same path back to trailhead.

18 Pigeon Spring Loop

This hike on the north slopes of Four Peaks passes through the remains of a large stand of ponderosa pine burned in the 60,000-acre Lone Fire in 1996. Although most of the big trees are gone, many other plants are making a comeback. There are two seasonal springs along this route.

Start: About 30 miles northeast of Mesa
Distance: 3.2-mile loop
Approximate hiking time: 2–3 hours
Elevation change: 860 feet
Difficulty: Easy due to short distance and little elevation change
Seasons: Spring through fall
Trail surface: Dirt and rocks
Water: Seasonally at Pigeon and Bear Springs
Other trail users: Horses

Land status: Four Peaks Wilderness, Tonto National Forest
Nearest town: Mesa
Fees and permits: Group size limited to 15; stay limit 14 days.
Maps: USGS Four Peaks; Trail Illustrated Superstition and Four Peaks Wildernesses; USFS Tonto National Forest
Trail contact: Mesa Ranger District, Tonto National Forest

Finding the trailhead: From Mesa, drive northeast on Highway 87. At Shea Boulevard, note your mileage, and continue 14 miles to Forest Road 143. Turn right onto this maintained dirt road, which becomes unmaintained and much rougher after 6.7 miles. When you are 18.3 miles from the highway, turn right onto Forest Road 648 and continue 0.5 mile south to the Pigeon Spring Trailhead. GPS: N33 42.65' W111 20.19'

The Hike

This is an interesting hike on a segment of the Arizona Trail through the heart of the Lone Fire burn. Watch out for unstable burned trees, which can fall at any time. Follow the trail, an old road, downhill 0.1 mile to Pigeon Spring, a masonry trough. Here the trail turns south and climbs over a saddle strewn with granite boulders. Thanks to the fire, there's a great view of Four Peaks from this minor pass. From here the trail drops slightly and crosses a drainage, then begins to climb gradually along the slopes at the head of Rock Creek. In the drainage below Bear Spring, you may find seasonal water, which sometimes forms a small cascade over the granite cliffs below the trail. As the trail crosses ravines and climbs around ridges, you'll pass though stands of pine that were mostly untouched by the Lone Fire, and then back into areas where every scrap of vegetation burned. The Pigeon Spring Trail ends at the junction with the Four Peaks Trail just after crossing a ravine.

Turn right and follow the Four Peaks Trail as it climbs steeply up the ravine. Abruptly the trail swings west and levels off. After the Four Peaks Trail swings around a ridge, the Amethyst Trail goes uphill to the left. Continue to contour on the Four Peaks Trail, which passes Bear Spring in another 0.5 mile. The trail ends at the Lone

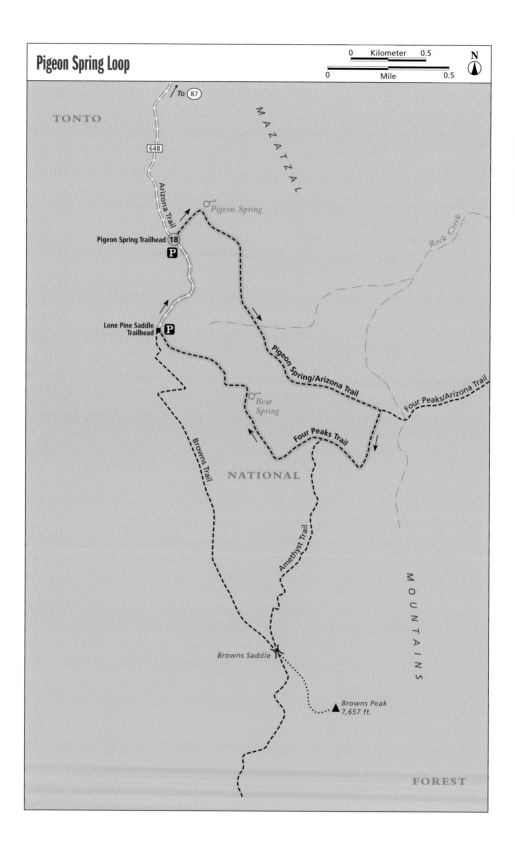

Pigeon Spring Loop

0 Kilometer 0.5

0 Mile 0.5

N

TONTO

To 87

648

Arizona Trail

Pigeon Spring

Pigeon Spring Trailhead 18

P

Lone Pine Saddle Trailhead

P

MAZATZAL

Rock Creek

Pigeon Spring/Arizona Trail

Four Peaks/Arizona Trail

Bear Spring

Four Peaks Trail

Browns Trail

NATIONAL

Amethyst Trail

MOUNTAINS

Browns Saddle

Browns Peak
7,657 ft.

FOREST

Browns Peak towers over granite boulders on the Pigeon Spring Loop.

Pine Saddle Trailhead, which was spared most of the devastation of the surrounding area. Now walk north on the road to reach Pigeon Spring Trailhead and your vehicle.

Miles and Directions

0.0 Begin at Pigeon Spring Trailhead.

0.2 Follow trail south at Pigeon Spring.

0.5 Reach saddle.

0.9 Arrive at drainage below Bear Spring.

1.4 Four Peaks Trail junction; turn right.

1.8 Amethyst Trail junction; continue on Four Peaks Trail.

2.3 Pass Bear Spring.

2.8 Pass Lone Pine Saddle Trailhead.

3.2 Return to Pigeon Spring Trailhead.

FIRE ON FOUR PEAKS

The early summer of 1996 was extremely dry, and when a careless, ignorant camper abandoned a campfire near Pigeon Spring, it soon exploded into a raging wildfire that incinerated 60,000 acres. The fire burned out of control for six days, and it took the efforts of hundreds of firefighters to contain. It's humbling to realize that a few coals from a campfire grew to become one of Arizona's largest wildfires. Though the Lone Fire is certainly the most devastating wildfire to occur in the Four Peaks area, the steep, dry mountains, rising directly out of the desert, have always had serious wildfires. Amazingly, though, pockets of Douglas fir and ponderosa pine have survived all of the fires. And within the heavily burned areas, vegetation is rapidly making a comeback, aided by a couple of wet winters and the very wet summer of 1999. After a wet season, wildflowers cover the burn in stretches of bright color.

GREEN TIP

Observe wildlife from a distance. Don't interfere in
their lives—both of you will be better for it.

Superstition Mountains

The Superstition Mountains are a small but rugged range lying east of Apache Junction, south of the Salt River, and trending west to east. Some Precambrian granite is exposed, especially in the eastern sections, but most of the Superstitions are a complex of interleaved lava flows, ash layers, and other volcanic deposits. Though the geology is difficult to decipher, the result is a spectacular and convoluted terrain of canyons, mesas, bluffs, and peaks. The potential for exploration is much greater than the size of the range would suggest. The western third of the range consists of high ridges, mesas, and deep canyons, ranging from 2,000 to 5,000 feet. Saguaro cactus and other Sonoran Desert plants grow on the lower slopes, while the higher country is a desert grassland with an occasional pinyon pine or juniper tree. Eastward the terrain becomes higher and somewhat gentler, though still complex. The eastern third of the range is dominated by deep canyons and high ridges and culminates in 6,266-foot Mound Mountain, the highest point in the Superstition Mountains. Chaparral brush (an association of scrub oak, mountain mahogany, and manzanita brush) covers the highest slopes, and a few pockets of stately ponderosa pine hang on in the coolest, most-protected locations.

Towering cliffs hem in Rogers Canyon just upstream from Angel Basin.

19 Western Foothills

This hike wanders along the base of the Superstition Mountains' western escarpment, using the Crosscut and Siphon Draw Trails, and offers some amazing views. Towering cliffs rise up from the desert slopes to the east, forming the famous skyline visible from Tempe, Mesa, Chandler, and the other eastern cities in the greater Phoenix area. As Superstition hikes go, this is an easy one.

Start: About 6 miles east of Apache Junction
Distance: 8.2 miles out and back
Approximate hiking time: 5 hours
Elevation change: 580 feet
Difficulty: Moderate due to distance and elevation change
Seasons: Fall through spring
Trail surface: Dirt and rocks
Water: None
Other trail users: Horses

Land status: Superstition Wilderness, Tonto National Forest
Nearest town: Apache Junction
Fees and permits: Group size limited to 15; stay limit 14 days.
Maps: USGS Goldfield; Trail Illustrated Superstition and Four Peaks Wildernesses; USFS Superstition Wilderness, USFS Tonto National Forest
Trail contact: Mesa Ranger District, Tonto National Forest

Finding the trailhead: From U.S. Highway 60 (Superstition Freeway) in Apache Junction, exit at Highway 88 (Idaho Road). Turn left onto Idaho Road, go 1.9 miles, then turn right onto Old West Highway. Continue 0.6 mile, then turn left onto East Broadway Avenue and drive 3.5 miles east to the East Broadway Trailhead. Parking is very limited. GPS: N33 24.47' W111 28.58'

The Hike

Follow the Crosscut Trail up the broad desert slope toward the imposing cliffs of the western escarpment of the Superstition Mountains. This type of slope is known as a bajada. It's composed of outwash debris—boulders, gravel, and sand—eroded from the steep mountains above and transported by flash floods out onto the plains. As the mountains erode, the debris piles up at their feet, forming a sloping skirtlike base.

As the trail nears the base of the cliffs, it turns north and contours across the mouth of Monument Canyon. Monument Canyon is an interesting cross-country side hike. Continuing north, the Crosscut Trail stays more or less level, high on the bajada, as it swings in and out of ravines. On a clear day, the Salt River Valley and greater Phoenix are laid out before you on the west, while the Superstition cliffs

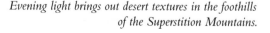

Evening light brings out desert textures in the foothills of the Superstition Mountains.

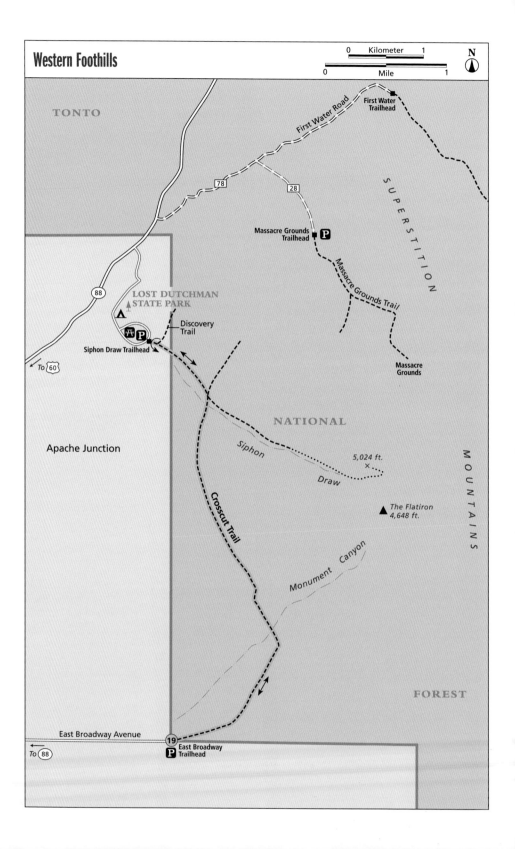

Western Foothills

0 ——— Kilometer ——— 1

0 ——— Mile ——— 1

N

TONTO

SUPERSTITION

First Water Road

First Water
Trailhead

78

28

Massacre Grounds
Trailhead P

Massacre Grounds Trail

88

LOST DUTCHMAN
STATE PARK

Discovery
Trail

P

Siphon Draw Trailhead

To 60

Massacre
Grounds

Apache Junction

NATIONAL

Siphon

Draw

5,024 ft.
×

M
O
U
N
T
A
I
N
S

The Flatiron
4,648 ft.

Crosscut Trail

Monument Canyon

FOREST

East Broadway Avenue

19

To 88

P East Broadway
Trailhead

loom over your right shoulder. Eventually the trail passes the mouth of Siphon Draw, then meets the Siphon Draw Trail at 3.4 miles. Turn left here and continue to Lost Dutchman State Park and the Siphon Draw Trailhead. Unless you're shuttling, return the way you came.

Miles and Directions

0.0 Begin at East Broadway Trailhead.

1.4 Reach mouth of Monument Canyon.

3.4 Siphon Draw Trail junction; turn left.

4.1 Arrive at Siphon Draw Trailhead.

8.2 Retrace your steps to return to East Broadway Trailhead.

GREEN TIP

Keep to established trails as much as possible. If there aren't any, stay on surfaces that will be least affected, like rock, gravel, or sand.

20 Siphon Draw

The hike up Siphon Draw follows a rugged trail, then ascends cross-country to the crest of Superstition Mountain. Once on the crest, you'll enjoy 100-mile views to the west and south and close-up views of much of the western Superstition Mountains. As close as it is to the cities of the Valley of the Sun, the crest still has a wild, remote feel, especially as one contemplates the deep canyons, mesas, and peaks spread out to the east.

Start: About 5 miles east of Apache Junction

Distance: 5.0 miles out and back

Approximate hiking time: 4-5 hours

Elevation change: 2,900 feet

Difficulty: Strenuous due to distance and elevation change

Seasons: Fall through spring

Trail surface: Dirt and rocks, cross-country

Water: None

Other trail users: Horses on the lower part of the trail

Land status: Superstition Wilderness, Tonto National Forest

Nearest town: Apache Junction

Fees and permits: Group size limited to 15; stay limit 14 days. Trailhead parking requires an entrance fee.

Maps: USGS Goldfield; Trail Illustrated Superstition and Four Peaks Wildernesses; USFS Superstition Wilderness, USFS Tonto National Forest

Trail contact: Mesa Ranger District, Tonto National Forest

Finding the trailhead: From Apache Junction, drive about 5 miles east on Highway 88, then turn right into Lost Dutchman State Park and follow the signs to the Siphon Draw Trailhead. GPS: N33 27.21' W111 28.80'

The Hike

Siphon Draw is the major canyon southeast of the state park. It's marked by The Flatiron, a distinctive rock formation south of the draw near the crest. The trail, wanders southeast across the desert foothills, at first climbing gradually toward the mouth of the canyon. You'll pass the Discovery Trail just after leaving the trailhead and cross the Crosscut Trail soon after. Once past the wilderness boundary, the gradient begins to steepen, and the impressive canyon walls and towering rock formations begin to close in. You'll also see fine examples of the stately saguaro cactus, the symbol of the Sonoran Desert, which grows up to 50 feet. The official, maintained trail ends here. Continue cross-country up the canyon, where you'll find a nonmaintained trail. Persist and you'll reach the crest of the western Superstitions, a high ridge commonly

Siphon Draw is one of several rugged canyons that cut into the ridge line of the western Superstition Mountains.

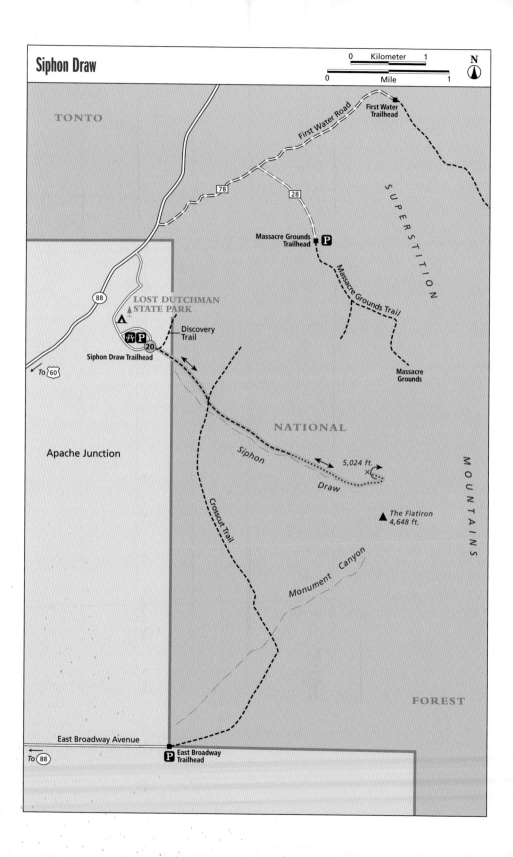

Siphon Draw

0 Kilometer 1
0 Mile 1

N

TONTO

First Water Road

First Water
Trailhead

78

28

Massacre Grounds
Trailhead

P

S
U
P
E
R
S
T
I
T
I
O
N

Massacre Grounds Trail

88

LOST DUTCHMAN
STATE PARK

Discovery
Trail

P

20

Siphon Draw Trailhead

Massacre
Grounds

To 60

Apache Junction

NATIONAL

Siphon

Draw

5,024 ft.
X

The Flatiron
4,648 ft.

M
O
U
N
T
A
I
N
S

Crosscut Trail

Monument Canyon

FOREST

East Broadway Avenue

To 88

P East Broadway
   Trailhead

SAGUARO, A DESERT SYMBOL

Saguaro cactus are often erroneously featured in images of the Great Basin, Mojave, and Chihuahuan Deserts, but they are found only in the Sonoran Desert in central and southern Arizona and northwestern Mexico, and there only where freezing temperatures are rare. A tough, waxy skin and an array of sharp spines protect the succulent, fleshy interior. They're supported by woody ribs just under the skin, which form cactus skeletons after they die. As they grow, saguaros usually develop several branching arms, which may help the plant maintain its balance. Large saguaros weigh several tons and get no support at all from their roots. The roots are shallow and spread out just below the surface in order to collect as much moisture as possible from the occasional rains. The volume of the cactus changes with the amount of moisture it has stored—you can see the depth of the accordion pleats in its skin changes from year to year. In the spring of wet years, the cactus produces a large, showy off-white flower at the tips of its stems.

referred to as "Superstition Mountain." This 5,000-foot ridge separates the urban world to the west from the wild and broken country to the east. The crest is high desert grassland, where scattered juniper trees start to appear. You can hike cross-country north or south along the crest from the head of Siphon Draw.

Miles and Directions

0.0 Begin at Siphon Draw Trailhead.

0.7 Crosscut Trail junction; continue straight ahead.

1.5 Wilderness boundary; begin cross-country hiking on informal trail.

2.5 Arrive at Superstition Mountain.

5.0 Return to trailhead.

Option

Lost Dutchman State Park features a small trail system in the park and along the foothills. Refer to the park trail map for information.

21 Massacre Grounds

This easy hike through the desert foothills of the western Superstition Mountains leads to a famous location where Spanish miners were supposedly ambushed and relieved of their newly found gold. Suitable for beginners and families, it makes an excellent introduction to hiking in the Superstition Mountains.

Start: About 7 miles northeast of Apache Junction

Distance: 3.0 miles out and back

Approximate hiking time: 2 hours

Elevation change: 810 feet

Difficulty: Easy due to short distance and little elevation change

Seasons: Fall through spring

Trail surface: Dirt and rocks

Water: None

Other trail users: Horses

Land status: Superstition Wilderness, Tonto National Forest

Nearest town: Apache Junction

Fees and permits: Group size limited to 15; stay limit 14 days.

Maps: USGS Goldfield; Trail Illustrated Superstition and Four Peaks Wildernesses; USFS Superstition Wilderness, USFS Tonto National Forest

Trail contact: Mesa Ranger District, Tonto National Forest

Finding the trailhead: From Apache Junction, drive 5.7 miles east on Arizona 88, then turn right on First Water Road (Forest Road 78). After 0.7 mile, park at the Jacob's Crosscut Trailhead (named Weekes Trailhead on some maps). GPS: N33° 28.30' W111° 28.17'

The Hike

From the trailhead, follow the First Water Road northeast to the old Massacre Grounds road, now closed. (There is no parking along First Water Road beyond the Jacob's Crosscut Trailhead.) Follow the old, closed road southeast toward the imposing cliffs of the northwest Superstitions. After you pass the old Massacre Grounds trailhead, the road becomes an informal trail which continues southeast toward the foot of the cliffs. The trail first passes to the west of a rocky bluff, then splits below a hill crowned with a rock pinnacle. Take the left fork. After about 1.5 miles, you'll reach the site of the massacre at the foot of the steep cliffs of Superstition Mountain. According to legend, Indians ambushed a group of Spanish miners in this area as they were returning to Mexico in 1848 with pack animals laden with gold ore. Despite the legend, and unfortunately for prospectors who believed it, gold has never been found in the Superstition Mountains. Regardless of its past, this area of the Superstition foothills is a special place, and it is especially delightful in spring after a wet winter

The Massacre Grounds at the northwestern corner of the Superstition
Mountains mark the site where a party of Spanish miners was killed.

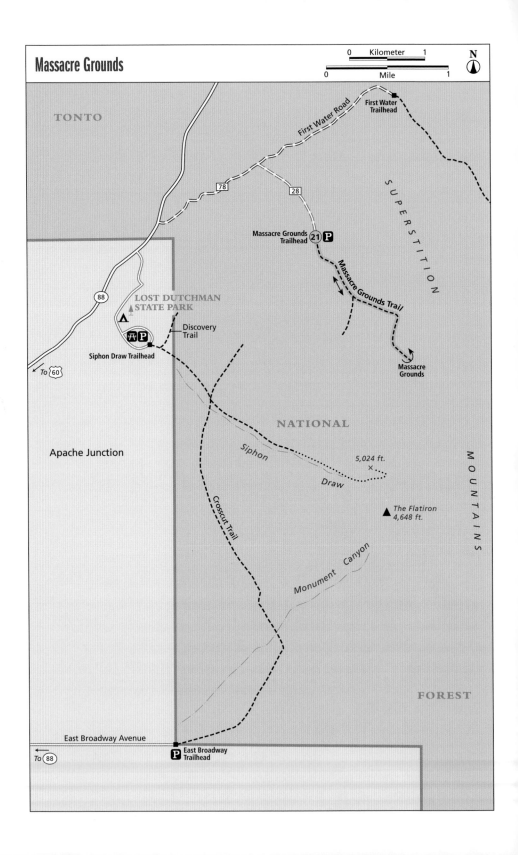

Massacre Grounds

0   Kilometer   1

0   Mile   1

N

TONTO

First Water Road

First Water
Trailhead

78

28

S U P E R S T I T I O N

Massacre Grounds
Trailhead

21 P

Massacre Grounds Trail

88

LOST DUTCHMAN
STATE PARK

Discovery
Trail

A P

Siphon Draw Trailhead

Massacre
Grounds

To 60

NATIONAL

Siphon

Draw

5,024 ft.
×

M O U N T A I N S

Apache Junction

The Flatiron
4,648 ft.

Crosscut Trail

Monument Canyon

FOREST

East Broadway Avenue

To 88

P East Broadway
Trailhead

when desert wildflowers carpet the hills. The dark, brooding cliffs of Superstition Mountain complete the scene.

Miles and Directions

0.0 Begin at Massacre Grounds Trailhead.

1.5 Arrive at Massacre Grounds.

3.0 Return to trailhead.

GREEN TIP

Don't take souvenirs home with you. This means natural materials such as plants, rocks, shells, and driftwood as well as historic artifacts such as fossils and arrowheads.

22 Garden Valley Loop

For those hikers who want to penetrate a little deeper into the Superstition Mountains, this moderate walk offers a glimpse of the mesas, buttes, and deep canyons lying at the heart of these desert mountains. Especially striking are the stone towers, or hoodoos, found in the vicinity of Parker Pass. These formations reveal the violent volcanic past of the Superstitions.

Start: About 8 miles northeast of Apache Junction

Distance: 8.8-mile loop

Approximate hiking time: 5 hours

Elevation change: 1,210 feet

Difficulty: Moderate due to distance and elevation change

Seasons: Fall through spring

Trail surface: Dirt and rocks

Water: None

Other trail users: Horses

Land status: Superstition Wilderness, Tonto National Forest

Nearest town: Apache Junction

Fees and permits: Group size limited to 15; stay limit 14 days.

Maps: USGS Goldfield; Trail Illustrated Superstition and Four Peaks Wildernesses; USFS Superstition Wilderness, USFS Tonto National Forest

Trail contact: Mesa Ranger District, Tonto National Forest

Finding the trailhead: From Apache Junction, drive 5.5 miles east on Highway 88, then turn right onto First Water Road (Forest Road 78). Continue 2.6 miles to the end of the road at the First Water Trailhead. GPS: N33 28.80' W111 26.58'

The Hike

Start off on the Dutchmans Trail, which heads southeast and soon enters a shallow canyon. This section of trail is a very easy and popular hike—don't expect solitude. But most people just walk a short distance up the trail, then turn back. Almost immediately, you'll pass the Second Water Trail, which is the return. Keep going, and you'll soon get a hint of the wilder side of the Superstitions. The trail wanders through low rock formations and past stands of cholla cactus, then climbs gently over Parker Pass, the broad divide between the First Water Canyon and Boulder Canyon drainages. Now you'll head more easterly, and the trail will gradually drop into Boulder Basin. This open valley is named for the huge quantity of boulders brought down by West Boulder Canyon, which drains the area south of you. Just before the trail crosses the main wash, turn left onto Black Mesa Trail. This trail heads northwest and climbs onto Black Mesa, passing west of Yellow Peak. Black Mesa's dark and stony surface is the result of a lava flow. After the short but steep initial climb, the trail ascends at a moderate grade toward a shallow saddle, which is the high point of the hike. Beyond the saddle, the Black Mesa Trail descends a shallow canyon, then comes out onto the open

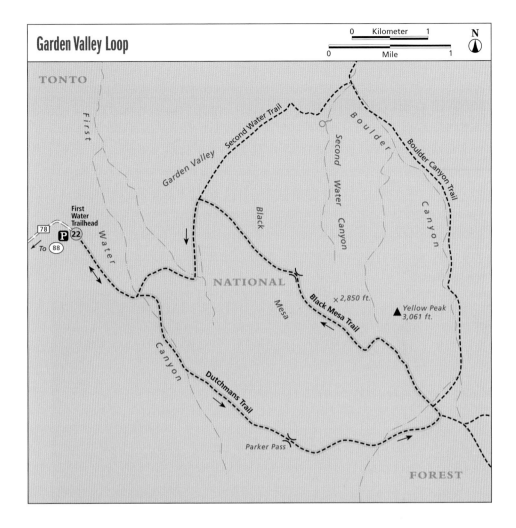

Garden Valley Loop

0   Kilometer   1

0   Mile   1

N

TONTO

First

Garden Valley   Second Water Trail

First
Water
Trailhead

78   P 22

To 88

Water

Black

Second

Water   Canyon

Boulder

Boulder Canyon Trail

Canyon

NATIONAL

Mesa

Black Mesa Trail   × 2,850 ft.

Yellow Peak
3,061 ft.

Canyon

Dutchmans Trail

Parker Pass

FOREST

flat of Garden Valley. You'll meet the Second Water Trail at a T intersection; turn left and head southwest. The trail soon descends off the rim of Black Mesa, following an old jeep road. It crosses a tributary of First Water Canyon, then swings west to meet the Dutchmans Trail and the return to First Water Trailhead.

Miles and Directions

0.0 Begin at First Water Trailhead.

0.8 Second Water Trail junction; stay right.

2.5 Cross Parker Pass.

4.0 Boulder Basin; turn left onto Black Mesa Trail.

5.8 Reach saddle on Black Mesa.

6.8 Garden Valley; turn left onto Second Water Trail.

7.5 Cross tributary of First Water Canyon.

8.0 Dutchmans Trail junction; turn right.

8.8 Return to First Water Trailhead.

HITCHIN' A RIDE—ON YOU?

Cholla cactus, like many other desert plants, is one you don't want to mess with. There are many varieties, but one of the best known is the teddy bear cholla, named for its cuddly appearance. This yellow-gold plant commonly grows about 2 to 4 feet high, and its stems are covered with a dense "fur" of sharp needles. Each needle is covered with tiny barbs. The stems are jointed, and as the plant grows, the tips of the stems break off and fall to the ground. When an animal or hiker brushes one of these fuzzy balls, it sticks to the skin or clothing and hitches a ride to another place, where, if conditions are favorable, a new cactus may germinate.

Sharp, barbed spines protect cholla cactus from animals.

23 Second Water Trail

This hike crosses Black Mesa and passes through Garden Valley on its way to Boulder Canyon, a major drainage in the western portion of the Superstition Mountains. Second Water Spring, a typical seasonal desert spring, is located just off the trail near its end. Boulder Canyon itself may be bone dry, especially during summer and late fall, or may be a flowing stream during periods of wet winter weather.

Start: About 8 miles northeast of Apache Junction

Distance: 7.6 miles out and back

Approximate hiking time: 4 hours

Elevation change: 630 feet

Difficulty: Moderate due to distance and elevation change

Seasons: Fall through spring

Trail surface: Dirt and rocks

Water: Seasonal in Second Water Canyon

Other trail users: Horses

Land status: Superstition Wilderness, Tonto National Forest

Nearest town: Apache Junction

Fees and permits: Group size limited to 15; stay limit 14 days.

Maps: USGS Goldfield; Trail Illustrated Superstition and Four Peaks Wildernesses; USFS Superstition Wilderness, USFS Tonto National Forest

Trail contact: Mesa Ranger District, Tonto National Forest

Finding the trailhead: From Apache Junction, drive 5.5 miles east on Highway 88, then turn right onto First Water Road (Forest Road 78). Continue 2.6 miles to the end of the road at the First Water Trailhead. GPS: N33 28.80' W111 26.58'

The Hike

After a short section on the Dutchmans Trail, take the Second Water Trail east toward Black Mesa, the low volcanic mesa east of the trailhead area. The trail climbs onto the mesa following a former jeep road, then passes a low hill on the right and enters the broad expanse of Garden Valley. At the junction with the Black Mesa Trail in Garden Valley, continue straight ahead (northeast) on the Second Water Trail, across the valley. The valley slopes gently down to the northeast, and shortly the trail enters a narrow canyon and starts to descend more rapidly. After an old bulldozer track branches to the left (it goes north to Cholla Tank, an old stock pond), the Second Water Trail becomes even steeper. Second Water Canyon enters from the right; Second Water Spring is a short distance up this side canyon. There is usually water in the canyon below the spring, which the trail follows to reach Boulder Canyon, the destination for our hike. This rugged canyon is dry most of the year, but it drains much of the western portion of the Superstition Mountains, and after heavy rains, it can be an uncrossable torrent. After gentle winter rains, you're more likely to find a clear, tumbling mountain stream, bordered by green grass and colorful flowers.

A hiker sets up camp in Boulder Canyon, near the end of the Second Water Trail.

WATER-MAKING THE MOST OF IT

The Sonoran Desert, an area encompassing the southwestern third of Arizona, Sonora State in northwest Mexico, and a bit of southeast California, is the most lush of the four North American deserts. Two rainy seasons provide the moisture to make this happen: Winter storms bring periods of gentle rain from December through March, and in late July the North American Monsoon brings scattered thunderstorms. Of course, the amount of precipitation in these rainy seasons varies widely from year to year and from place to place. But desert plants and animals have adapted well to unpredictable moisture and desert extremes of drought and heat. For example, wildflower seeds are capable of lying dormant within the soil for many years until the right combination of moisture and temperature triggers their germination. And plants take advantage of the unusual moisture supply to quickly complete their life cycle, so that by the time summer's heat arrives, new seeds ensure the next generation of plants. This rush to flower, be pollinated, and secure a continuing place in the landscape is the reason for the desert's famed, spectacular displays of blooms.

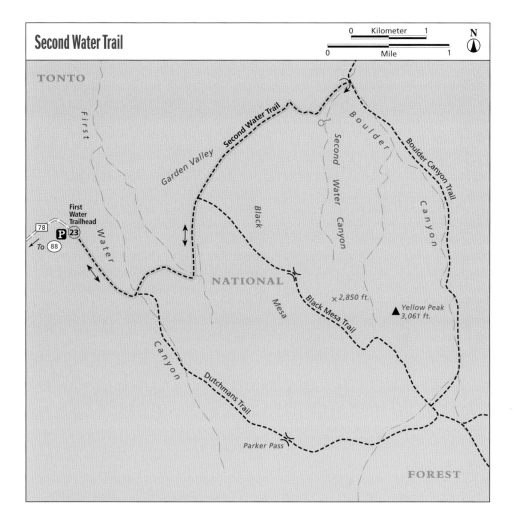

Second Water Trail

Miles and Directions

0.0   Begin at First Water Trailhead.

2.1   Black Mesa Trail junction; stay left.

3.5   Reach Second Water Spring, up canyon to the south.

3.8   Arrive at Boulder Canyon.

7.6   Return to trailhead via the same route.

24 Lower La Barge Box

Starting from one of the most accessible of the Superstition Wilderness trailheads, near Canyon Lake, this exceptionally scenic cross-country hike takes you into a classic "box" canyon. Towering walls and seasonal pools of water add to the charm of this remote spot.

Start: About 15 miles northeast of Apache Junction

Distance: 11.0 miles out and back

Approximate hiking time: 6–7 hours

Elevation change: 1,840 feet

Difficulty: Moderate due to distance and elevation change

Seasons: Fall through spring

Trail surface: Dirt and rocks

Water: Seasonal in La Barge Creek

Other trail users: Horses on the trail portion of the hike

Land status: Superstition Wilderness, Tonto National Forest

Nearest town: Apache Junction

Fees and permits: Group size limited to 15; stay limit 14 days.

Maps: USGS Mormon Flat Dam and Goldfield; Trail Illustrated Superstition and Four Peaks Wildernesses; USFS Superstition Wilderness, USFS Tonto National Forest

Trail contact: Mesa Ranger District, Tonto National Forest

Finding the trailhead: From Apache Junction, drive about 14.5 miles east on Highway 88 to Canyon Lake Marina. Signed trailhead parking is on the left in the marina parking lot. GPS: N33 32.09' W111 25.35'

The Hike

Cross the highway and start up the Boulder Canyon Trail, which climbs steadily southeast up the ridge above Boulder Canyon. A spur trail soon branches right and descends to La Barge Canyon, but stay left on the Boulder Canyon Trail, which continues to climb via a switchback or two, then levels out along the top of the ridge. Look behind you at the expansive view of Canyon Lake and the Four Peaks region. Now the trail contours high above Boulder Canyon and soon leaves the sights and sounds of the man-made lake behind. Rounding a rock spur, the trail drops steeply into La Barge Creek. This is a popular destination for both day hikes and overnight hikes, and there's usually water in the creek during the cool half of the year.

Follow the main trail across La Barge Creek, then upstream. When the trail turns right and climbs away from the creek, leave it and continue cross-country up the canyon. At first, the going is easy up the broad wash, but as you enter Lower La Barge Box, the walls close in and travel becomes more difficult. At several places, you'll have to scramble up and around huge boulders. The most impressive section of the canyon begins where there is a sharp left bend, followed by a sharp right bend. Here the walls seem to go straight up. The narrows continue for about a mile, then the canyon

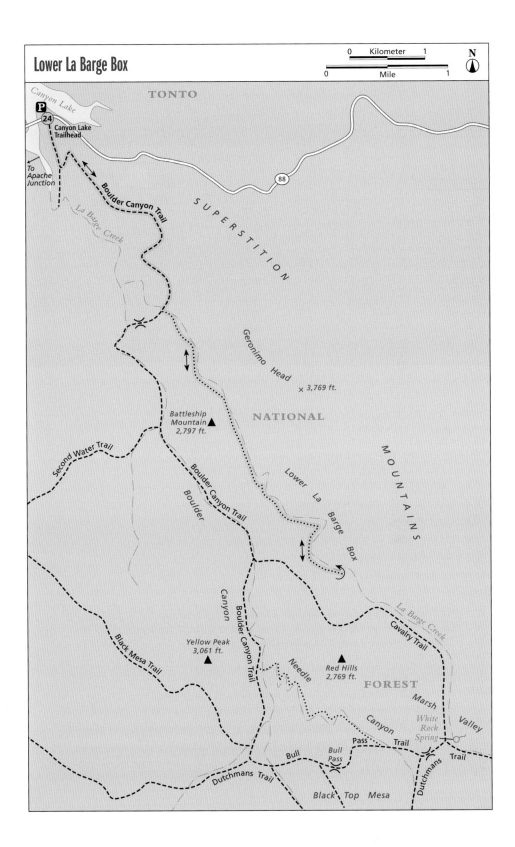

Lower La Barge Box

TONTO

Canyon Lake

P
24

Canyon Lake
Trailhead

To
Apache
Junction

S U P E R S T I T I O N

88

Boulder Canyon Trail

La Barge Creek

Geronimo Head

× 3,769 ft.

NATIONAL

Battleship
Mountain
2,797 ft. ▲

Second Water Trail

Boulder Canyon Trail

Boulder

Lower La Barge Box

M O U N T A I N S

Canyon

Boulder Canyon Trail

La Barge Creek

Cavalry Trail

Black Mesa Trail

Yellow Peak
3,061 ft. ▲

Needle

Red Hills
2,769 ft. ▲

FOREST

Marsh

White
Rock
Spring

Valley

Canyon
Pass

Trail

Trail

Dutchmans

Bull
Pass

Bull

Dutchmans Trail

Black Top Mesa

0   Kilometer   1

0   Mile   1

N

Canyon Lake forms the scenic backdrop during the hike up the first section of La Barge Trail.

suddenly opens up, marking the upper end of Lower La Barge Box. This is the turn-around point for our hike.

Miles and Directions

0.0   Begin at Canyon Lake Trailhead.

0.4   Spur trail junction; continue on main trail.

0.9   Cross ridgetop.

2.4   La Barge Creek; leave trail and hike cross-country up La Barge Creek.

5.5   Arrive at Lower La Barge Box.

11.0   Return to trailhead.

Option

For a much shorter and easier hike, take the unsigned spur trail near the beginning of the Boulder Canyon Trail. This trail ends in the bed of lower La Barge Creek, not too far from Canyon Lake. The round-trip hike is 3.0 miles.

INSIDE THE BOX

A box canyon is a canyon that has a narrow section bounded by tall cliffs and generally some obstacle in the bed that makes it difficult to traverse, especially on horseback. Sometimes the obstacle is a high, dry waterfall, or as in the case of Lower La Barge Box, the canyon floor may be choked with boulders. Obviously, a box canyon is not the place to be during a flash flood.

25 Marsh Valley Loop

This is an enjoyable hike through the middle section of Boulder Canyon and the lower end of La Barge Canyon—two of the most rugged canyons in the Superstition Mountains. The transition between the canyons traverses Marsh Valley, a rare open valley in this wilderness of deep canyons, high cliffs, and towering buttes. Several options for side hikes extend the trip for those who want to explore more of the area.

Start: About 8 miles northeast of Apache Junction

Distance: 16.4-mile loop

Approximate hiking time: 12 hours or 2 days

Elevation change: 3,910 feet

Difficulty: Strenuous due to distance and elevation change

Seasons: Fall through spring

Trail surface: Dirt and rocks

Water: Seasonal in La Barge and Boulder Creeks, and at White Rock Spring

Other trail users: Horses

Land status: Superstition Wilderness, Tonto National Forest

Nearest town: Apache Junction

Fees and permits: Group size limited to 15; stay limit 14 days.

Maps: USGS Mormon Flat Dam and Goldfield; Trail Illustrated Superstition and Four Peaks Wildernesses; USFS Superstition Wilderness, USFS Tonto National Forest

Trail contact: Mesa Ranger District, Tonto National Forest

Finding the trailhead: From Apache Junction, drive about 14.5 miles east on Highway 88 to Canyon Lake Marina. Signed trailhead parking is on the left in the marina parking lot. GPS: N33 32.09' W111 25.35'

The Hike

Cross the highway and follow the Boulder Canyon Trail over the ridge into La Barge Canyon. Follow the trail across the creek and upstream a short distance, where the trail turns west and climbs over a low pass into Boulder Canyon. Both La Barge and Boulder Canyons have seasonal water. When the Boulder Canyon Trail reaches Boulder Canyon, turn left and follow the trail up the broad, boulder-filled wash. You'll pass the junction with the Second Water Trail on the right; there is seasonal water in Second Water Canyon. Continue south on the Boulder Canyon Trail, then turn left onto the Cavalry Trail, which climbs steeply out of Boulder Canyon and over a pass into La Barge Creek. The trail turns right and goes southeast up Marsh Valley and ends at the Dutchmans Trail at the head of the valley. White Rock Spring usually has water.

Turn right onto the Dutchmans Trail and follow it a short distance to a low pass, then turn right onto the Bull Pass Trail to continue the loop. The trail drops a short distance into Needle Canyon, then crosses the wash and starts to climb steeply along the north slopes of Black Top Mesa. You'll reach the high point of the hike at Bull

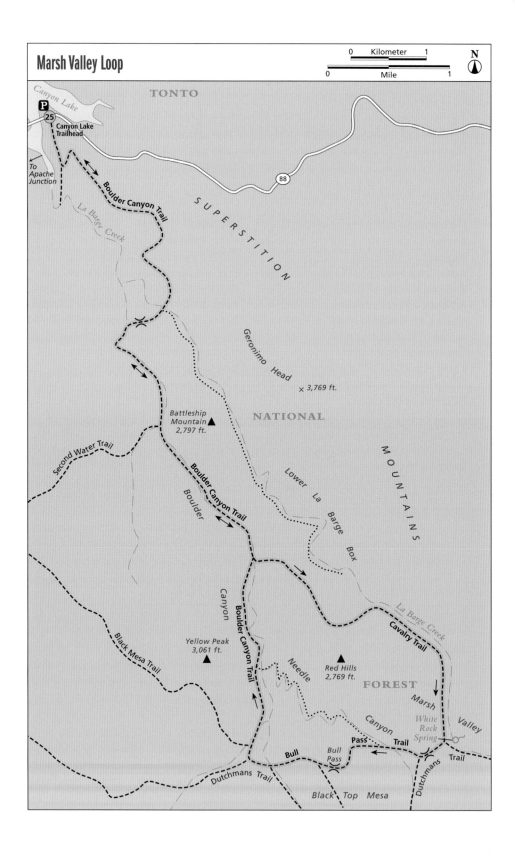

Marsh Valley Loop

0 ——— Kilometer ——— 1

0 ——— Mile ——— 1

N

TONTO

Canyon Lake

P 25

Canyon Lake
Trailhead

To
Apache
Junction

Boulder Canyon Trail

La Barge Creek

88

SUPERSTITION

Geronimo Head
× 3,769 ft.

NATIONAL

Battleship
Mountain
2,797 ft.

Second Water Trail

Boulder Canyon Trail

Boulder

Lower La Barge Box

MOUNTAINS

Canyon

Boulder Canyon Trail

La Barge Creek

Cavalry Trail

Black Mesa Trail

Yellow Peak
3,061 ft.

Needle

Red Hills
2,769 ft.

FOREST

Marsh

Valley

White
Rock
Spring

Canyon

Trail

Dutchmans
Trail

Bull Pass

Bull
Pass

Dutchmans Trail

Black Top Mesa

Pass, and then drop steeply to rejoin the Boulder Canyon Trail in Boulder Canyon. Turn right and hike north down the canyon past the confluence with Needle Canyon, which is on the right. You'll pass the junction with the Cavalry Trail, completing the loop portion of the trip. Return to the Canyon Lake Trailhead via the Boulder Canyon Trail.

Miles and Directions

0.0   Begin at Canyon Lake Trailhead.

0.9   Reach the ridgetop.

2.4   Cross La Barge Creek—follow trail west out of La Barge Canyon.

2.7   Cross Boulder Creek.

3.7   Second Water Trail junction; continue up Boulder Canyon.

5.0   Cavalry Trail junction; turn left.

6.5   La Barge Creek joins trail to east at head of Marsh Valley.

7.9   Dutchmans Trail junction; turn right.

8.1   Bull Pass Trail junction; turn right.

9.0   Reach Bull Pass.

9.5   Boulder Canyon Trail junction; turn right.

11.4   Cavalry Trail junction; continue north on Boulder Canyon Trail.

12.7   Second Water Trail junction; continue north on Boulder Canyon Trail.

14.0   Cross La Barge Creek.

16.4   Return to Canyon Lake Trailhead.

Options

Option 1. When the Boulder Canyon Trail first reaches La Barge Creek, you could follow La Barge Creek cross-country upstream through Lower La Barge Box and join the Cavalry Trail in Marsh Valley. This off-trail section is about 3.4 miles, and it shortens the loop by 0.8 mile, though it probably will take more time because of the rough cross-country hiking.

Option 2. Where the Bull Pass Trail crosses Needle Canyon, you could leave the trail and follow the canyon through its lower narrows. This cross-country hike is 1.6 miles, and it shortens the loop by 0.2 mile.

Option 3. If you don't take option 2, you can do a short but scenic side hike up an old trail to the top of Black Top Mesa, but again, your hiking time will be longer. This route leaves Bull Pass and climbs south about 0.6 mile to the south edge of the mesa, the high point. You may not find much of the trail, but the hiking is easy. From the end of this little side hike, you'll have a great view of Weavers Needle and the rugged country surrounding this famous landmark. Weavers Needle is probably named after Pauline Weaver, an early mountain man and fur trapper.

CANYON FLOOD, AWESOME AFTERMATH

Considering that little or no water flows through canyons such as Boulder Canyon most of the time, you might wonder how all those boulders got there. The secret is that Boulder Canyon drains a large area of the western Superstitions. Most storms produce only a small, fairly steady runoff, but occasionally a heavy rain occurs that causes a rapid runoff. The dry wash can become a raging torrent in a matter of seconds, as floodwaters gather from miles away and converge on the main drainage. Boulders that fell from the canyon walls and lay in the wash for many years suddenly find themselves buoyed by the massive force of the flood. The carrying capacity of moving water goes up with the cube of the velocity, so as a flow doubles in size, it becomes capable of moving much larger rocks. A huge flood in a canyon like Boulder Canyon is an unforgettable sight and sound, as rocks the size of small cars are jostled about.

26 Peters Mesa

The loop backpack trip over Peters Mesa takes you into a challenging but scenic portion of the north-central Superstition Wilderness. Additional attractions include Upper La Barge Box in the middle section of the loop and the opportunity to check out the narrow confines of well-named Trap Canyon.

Start: About 22 miles northeast of Apache Junction

Distance: 21.8-mile loop

Approximate hiking time: 12 hours or 2 days

Elevation change: 4,150 feet

Difficulty: Strenuous due to distance, elevation change, and faint trails

Seasons: Fall through spring

Trail surface: Dirt and rocks

Water: La Barge and Charlebois Springs are usually reliable; seasonal water at Upper La Barge Box, Trap Canyon Spring, Music Canyon Spring, and Kane Spring

Other trail users: Horses

Land status: Superstition Wilderness, Tonto National Forest

Nearest town: Apache Junction

Fees and permits: Group size limited to 15; stay limit 14 days.

Maps: USGS Horse Mesa Dam and Weavers Needle; Trail Illustrated Superstition and Four Peaks Wildernesses; USFS Superstition Wilderness, USFS Tonto National Forest

Trail contact: Mesa Ranger District, Tonto National Forest

Finding the trailhead: From Apache Junction, drive 20 miles east on Highway 88 to the end of the pavement. Continue another 2.3 miles on the gravel road to the Tortilla Trailhead, on the right. GPS: N33° 31.56' W 111° 19.15'

Special considerations: Although this hike is entirely on trail, some sections are faint and difficult to follow. You should have both the USGS topo maps and the USFS Superstition Wilderness map with you, as well as skill in route finding.

The Hike

Follow the old road south along the top of the ridge, then down into the Tortilla Creek drainage past the old Tortilla Ranch site to a trail junction near Tortilla Well. Turn left onto the JF Trail, which heads southeast up a gentle ridge. Watch for the sometimes-obscure junction with the Hoolie Bacon Trail, and turn right onto this trail, which takes you south off the ridge and into Tortilla Creek. Follow the trail upstream around a bend, where it leaves Tortilla Creek and climbs up a drainage, then continues southwest, climbing steadily. This section can be difficult to find. The trail is heading for a pass on Horse Ridge, ahead. After crossing the broad pass, the trail drops into Horse Camp Basin, which is the hilly confluence of several small drainages. Now the trail, still faint, turns south and drops into the Trap Canyon drainage. After crossing a tributary of Trap Canyon, the trail (incorrectly shown as the Peters Trail

95

Seasonal pools of water, like these in Peters Canyon, are critical sources of water for wildlife and backpackers alike.

on the USGS topographic map) turns farther left and heads southeast over a low pass next to the cliffs of Herman Mountain. (A branch of the Peters Trail shown on the USGS map heading northwest from here does not exist.) Finally, the trail drops into La Barge Canyon and meets the Red Tanks Trail.

Turn right and follow the Red Tanks Trail downstream into Upper La Barge Box, a spectacular canyon formed by the towering walls of Coffee Flat and Herman Mountains. There is often seasonal water in the creek here. When the trail emerges from the canyon, it meets the popular and well-traveled Whiskey Spring Trail. Turn right and follow it northwest down La Barge Creek past Trap Canyon. A side trail goes 0.2 mile to Trap Canyon Spring, which usually has water. La Barge Spring, which is more reliable, is located just before the junction with the heavily used Dutchmans Trail.

Turn right onto the Dutchmans Trail, which continues down La Barge Creek. Music Canyon Spring is another potential water source located 0.1 mile up a spur trail on the right (east). The next side canyon on the right is Charlebois Canyon; turn right here onto the Peters Trail. You'll pass Charlebois Spring (which is usually reliable) before the Peters Trail starts a steep climb south out of the canyon. After reaching a ridge, the trail swings east, then northwest into a small canyon to continue the climb over Peters Mesa. Watch carefully for cairns—some sections of the trail are faint and easily lost. After contouring around the head of a tributary of Charlebois Canyon, the Peters Trail continues a short distance northwest, then makes an abrupt turn east and climbs over a broad saddle on the crest of Peters Mesa. (The wilderness map shows an old trail heading west from this turning point, but only faint traces remain.) If you lose the trail in this area, head east toward the pass, and you should pick up the trail as it drops into Peters Canyon.

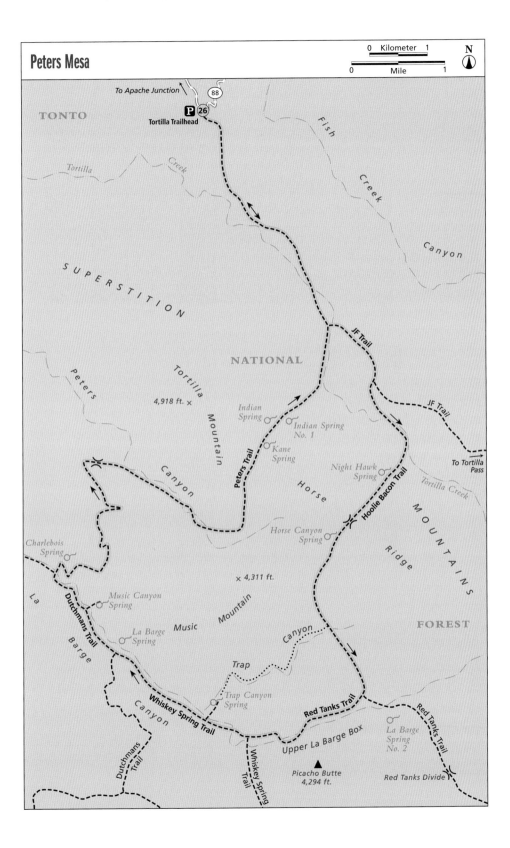

Peters Mesa

0 Kilometer 1
0 Mile 1

N

To Apache Junction

88

P 26
Tortilla Trailhead

TONTO

Tortilla   Creek

Fish   Creek   Canyon

S U P E R S T I T I O N

NATIONAL

JF Trail

JF Trail

Peters

Tortilla   Mountain

4,918 ft. ×

Indian
Spring

Indian Spring
No. 1

Kane
Spring

Night Hawk
Spring

To Tortilla
Pass

Peters Trail

Canyon

Horse

Tortilla Creek

Hoolie Bacon Trail

Horse Canyon
Spring

M O U N T A I N S

Charlebois
Spring

Ridge

× 4,311 ft.

La

Music Canyon
Spring

Dutchmans Trail

La Barge
Spring

Music   Mountain

FOREST

Barge

Canyon

Trap

Whiskey Spring Trail

Trap Canyon
Spring

Red Tanks Trail

Red Tanks Trail

La Barge
Spring
No. 2

Canyon

Dutchmans
Trail

Whiskey Spring
Trail

Upper La Barge Box

▲ Picacho Butte
4,294 ft.

Red Tanks Divide

Once in Peters Canyon, the trail follows the drainage upstream (southeast) for a little over a mile before climbing away from the bed to the east. Follow the trail through a saddle next to a low hill, and then northward. (The USGS topographic map shows a trail junction here, but the trail shown heading southeast no longer exists.) The Peters Trail climbs over a saddle at the point where Horse Ridge meets Tortilla Mountain, passes Kane Spring, then drops into a tributary of Tortilla Creek and follows the wash back to Tortilla Well. Now retrace your steps on the old Tortilla Ranch road to the Tortilla Trailhead off Highway 88.

Miles and Directions

0.0 Begin at Tortilla Trailhead—follow the old road south.

2.8 Tortilla Well—start on the JF Trail.

3.6 Hoolie Bacon Trail junction; turn right.

4.3 Cross Tortilla Creek.

5.8 Arrive at top of Horse Ridge.

7.7 Red Tanks Trail junction; turn right.

9.0 Whiskey Spring Trail junction; turn right.

10.9 Dutchmans Trail junction; turn right.

12.1 Peters Trail junction; turn right.

12.2 Pass Charlebois Spring.

14.3 Reach saddle of Peters Mesa.

17.3 Trail joins Tortilla Creek.

18.8 Pass Tortilla Well.

21.8 Return to Tortilla Trailhead.

Option

Where the Hoolie Bacon Trail crosses Trap Canyon, it's possible to leave the trail and hike directly down Trap Canyon to the spur trail at Trap Canyon Spring and on down to the Whiskey Spring Trail. It's about 1.8 miles to Trap Canyon Spring and another 0.2 mile to the Whiskey Spring Trail. This is a shortcut in distance only—the cross-country hike will take more time than the longer route on the trail. Be prepared to lower packs at several spots in this imposing and rough canyon. You might want to bring a 20- or 30-foot length of ¼-inch rope for this purpose.

ARIZONA'S STATE TREE

Along this hike, you'll see the Arizona state tree, the *palo verde*. The name means "green stick" in Spanish, which nicely describes this small desert tree. In order to survive long periods without water, the tree drops its leaves and depends on chlorophyll in its branches and stems to produce food. After spring rains, the tree quickly produces thousands of tiny leaves. If there's enough moisture, the tree becomes covered with a cloud of tiny yellow flowers, transforming the desert with its heady perfume.

27 Tortilla Pass–Red Tanks Divide

This hike is a classic backpack trip through remote and less-visited canyons in the central Superstition Mountains, including Fraser, Randolph, and Red Tanks Canyons. It includes a traverse of the high ridge between Fish Creek and upper Tortilla Creek, views of much of the Superstition Mountains, and a walk past the historic JF Ranch, a working cattle ranch on the southern edge of the Superstition Wilderness.

Start: About 22 miles northeast of Apache Junction

Distance: 26.4-mile loop

Approximate hiking time: 3 days

Elevation change: 5,410 feet

Difficulty: Strenuous due to distance, elevation change, and faint trails

Seasons: Fall through spring

Trail surface: Dirt and rocks

Water: Seasonal water at Mullin Spring, Dripping Spring, and Night Hawk Spring, and in Fraser Canyon, Randolph Canyon, and Upper La Barge Box. In dry years, you may have to carry extra water for camp along the first part of this loop.

Other trail users: Horses

Land status: Superstition Wilderness, Tonto National Forest

Nearest town: Apache Junction

Fees and permits: Group size limited to 15; stay limit 14 days.

Maps: USGS Horse Mesa Dam, Weavers Needle, and Iron Mountain; Trail Illustrated Superstition and Four Peaks Wildernesses; USFS Superstition Wilderness, USFS Tonto National Forest

Trail contact: Mesa Ranger District, Tonto National Forest

Finding the trailhead: From Apache Junction, drive 20 miles east on Highway 88 to the end of the pavement. Continue another 2.3 miles on the gravel road to the Tortilla Trailhead, on the right. GPS: N33° 31.56' W 111° 19.15'

You can also start this loop from the Woodbury Trailhead. From Apache Junction, drive 19 miles east on U.S. Highway 60, then turn left onto Queen Creek Road. Continue 2.4 miles on this paved road, then turn right on Forest Road 537, which is maintained dirt. Go 3.3 miles, then turn left onto Forest Road 172, the Hewlitt Canyon Road. This road is maintained, but you must cross Queen Creek at the start. If either Queen Creek or Hewlitt Canyon is flooding, this approach will be impassable. Continue 8.8 miles to a locked gate, then turn right and go 0.1 mile to the Woodbury Trailhead. GPS: N33° 24.85 W111° 12.36'

Hike 0.5 mile north on the JF Trail, then turn left onto the Woodbury Trail to start the loop at its southeast corner.

The Hike

Start by following the old Tortilla Ranch Road south along a ridge, then down into the Tortilla Creek drainage. After passing the Tortilla Ranch site, you'll reach a trail junction near Tortilla Well. Hike southeast on the JF Trail, which climbs gradually onto the unnamed ridge between Tortilla Creek and Lost Dutch Canyon. You'll pass the Hoolie Bacon Trail, which branches right and will be your return trail. As the JF Trail continues to work its way up the ridge, the terrain gradually becomes high desert grassland with expanding views of the central part of the Superstitions. Eventually you cross the highest point of the trail and the trip. The trail then drops slightly, crosses through a saddle, then swings into the head of Tortilla Creek. Here a side trail goes right about 0.5 mile to Mullin Spring. The main trail continues east to Tortilla Pass, where the Rogers Canyon Trail branches left. Turn right to stay on the JF Trail, which drops steeply south down a canyon. The trail finally drops into Randolph Canyon and follows the drainage upstream to the Woodbury Trail.

Turn right here and cross a broad saddle into Fraser Canyon. The trail passes the JF Ranch, then continues southwest down the canyon. There is seasonal water in the bed. When Fraser Canyon ends at Randolph Canyon, you are at the low point of the loop. Turn right onto the Red Tanks Trail and follow Randolph Canyon north, upstream. Watch for Red Tanks Canyon on the left; a short distance upstream, the Red Tanks Trail leaves Randolph Canyon on the left, climbs over a spur, and drops into Red Tanks Canyon. You may see traces of an old trail up Randolph Canyon—don't take this trail by mistake.

At first, the trail follows Red Tanks Canyon, which drains the imposing cliffs of Coffee Flat Mountain, towering above you to the west. Soon it veers left (west) up an unnamed side canyon and climbs over Red Tanks Divide. It's easy to lose the trail

Backpackers take a rest in La Barge Canyon.

Tortilla Pass-Red Tanks Divide

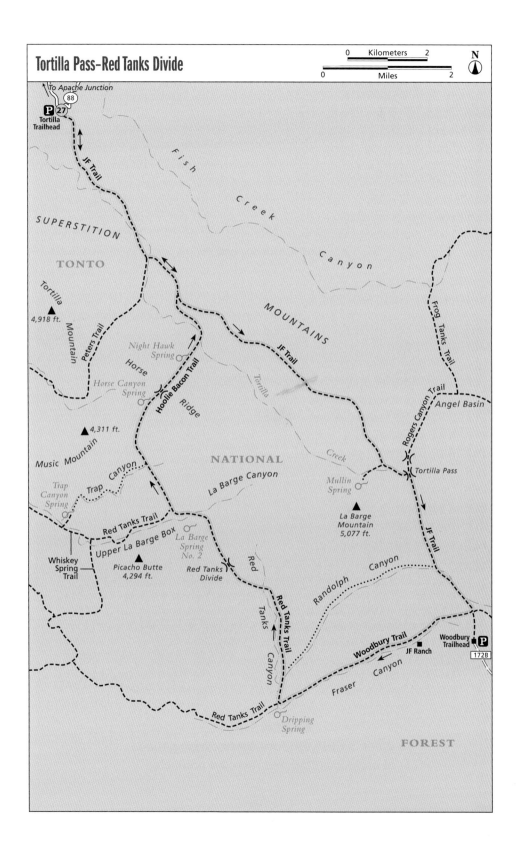

0   Kilometers   2

0   Miles   2

N

To Apache Junction

88

P 27
Tortilla
Trailhead

JF Trail

F i s h

C r e e k

C a n y o n

SUPERSTITION

TONTO

Tortilla
Mountain
4,918 ft.

Peters Trail

Night Hawk
Spring

Horse

Horse Canyon
Spring

Hoolie Bacon Trail

Ridge

M O U N T A I N S

JF Trail

Tortilla

Frog Tanks Trail

Rogers Canyon Trail

Angel Basin

4,311 ft.

Music Mountain

Trap
Canyon
Spring

Trap Canyon

Creek

NATIONAL

La Barge Canyon

Mullin
Spring

Tortilla Pass

JF Trail

La Barge
Mountain
5,077 ft.

Red Tanks Trail

Upper La Barge Box

Whiskey
Spring
Trail

Picacho Butte
4,294 ft.

La Barge
Spring
No. 2

Red Tanks
Divide

Red

Randolph   Canyon

Red Tanks Trail

Tanks

Canyon

Woodbury Trail

JF Ranch

Woodbury
Trailhead

P

172B

Fraser   Canyon

Red Tanks Trail

Dripping
Spring

FOREST

here, so you should have the Weavers Needle USGS map with you. North of the pass, the trail follows a drainage down to La Barge Creek and meets the Hoolie Bacon Trail just east of Upper La Barge Box. Turn right onto the Hoolie Bacon Trail, which can be difficult to follow through the next section.

The trail climbs north up a slope on the east side of Herman Mountain, crosses a broad pass, then drops slightly into Trap Canyon. Heading more northwesterly, it follows Trap Canyon for a short distance, then turns north and heads through Horse Camp Basin. Turning northeast, the trail climbs over Horse Ridge, then drops into Tortilla Creek. Turn left and follow the trail down Tortilla Creek about a mile. Watch for the point where the trail leaves the drainage on the right and climbs north to meet the JF Trail. Turn left onto the JF Trail at 22.8 miles to return to Tortilla Well, then retrace your steps on the old Tortilla Ranch Road to return to the Tortilla Trailhead on Highway 88.

Miles and Directions

0.0 Begin at Tortilla Trailhead.

2.8 Pass Tortilla Well.

3.6 Hoolie Bacon Trail junction; stay left on JF Trail.

8.8 Rogers Canyon Trail at Tortilla Pass; stay right on JF Trail.

11.2 Woodbury Trail junction; turn right.

14.6 Red Tanks Trail junction; turn right.

17.3 Arrive at Red Tanks Divide.

18.7 Hoolie Bacon Trail junction; turn right.

20.9 Ascend Horse Ridge.

21.8 Cross Tortilla Creek.

22.8 JF Trail junction; turn left.

23.6 Pass Tortilla Well.

26.4 Return to Tortilla Trailhead.

Options

Option 1. When you reach Randolph Canyon at the bottom of the descent from Tortilla Pass, turn right and hike cross-country down Randolph Canyon to Red Tanks Canyon. The going is easy, though you won't see much trace of the trail shown on the Weavers Needle USGS map. Although Randolph Canyon is a 1.6-mile shortcut, your hiking time will be about the same. There's seasonal water in the canyon.

Option 2. You can make this a longer loop (four to five days) by remaining on the Red Tanks Trail at the Hoolie Bacon Trail junction. Then use the Whiskey Spring, Dutchmans, and Peters Trails to complete the loop. (See the Peters Mesa hike for details.)

GREEN TIP
Be green and stylish too—wear clothing made
of organic cotton and recycled products.

28 Reavis Ranch

This popular hike follows the north end of the Reavis Ranch Trail to the historic Reavis Ranch, a former working cattle ranch in the heart of the Superstition Mountains. The old ranch headquarters area includes an apple orchard, which still produces fine fruit—a real treat after the long hike to the ranch site.

Start: About 30 miles northeast of Apache Junction

Distance: 21.2-mile out and back

Approximate hiking time: 11 hours or 2 days

Elevation change: 2,790 feet

Difficulty: Strenuous due to distance and elevation change

Seasons: Fall through spring

Trail surface: Dirt and rocks

Water: Seasonal at Plow Saddle Spring and in Reavis Creek south of the ranch site

Other trail users: Horses

Land status: Superstition Wilderness, Tonto National Forest

Nearest town: Apache Junction

Fees and permits: Group size limited to 15; stay limit 14 days.

Maps: USGS Pinyon Mountain and Iron Mountain; Trail Illustrated Superstition and Four Peaks Wildernesses; USFS Superstition Wilderness, USFS Tonto National Forest

Trail contact: Mesa Ranger District, Tonto National Forest

Finding the trailhead: From Apache Junction, drive 20 miles east on Highway 88 to the end of the pavement. Continue another 7.4 miles on the gravel road to Reavis Ranch Road (Forest Road 212) and then turn right. Now drive 3.0 miles to the Reavis Trailhead at the end of the road. GPS: N33° 33.38' W111° 15.55'

The Hike

The Reavis Ranch was the only ranch within the Superstition Wilderness when the wilderness area was established, and vehicle access to the ranch was via a long and winding road from Highway 88. After the USDA Forest Service bought the ranch, the ranch site and road corridor were added to the wilderness. Today the old road is maintained as a foot and horse trail, and the route makes a fine hike though the east-central portion of the Superstition Mountains.

The trail climbs steadily, at first heading east as it works its way along the complex ridge system north of Lewis and Pranty Creek. After several miles it swings south, around the head of the creek, and climbs towards Castle Dome, a prominent rounded peak. Note how the vegetation changes from low desert scrub to high desert grassland as you ascend. The old road skirts the peak on the east and climbs over an unnamed saddle, which is the highest elevation of the hike. Now you'll descend slightly and hike through Windy Pass at the head of Fish Creek Canyon. Turning more to the east, the trail passes through broad Plow Saddle and climbs over a ridge. It crosses another broad saddle at the head of Willow Creek; here the Frog Tanks Trail forks right. The

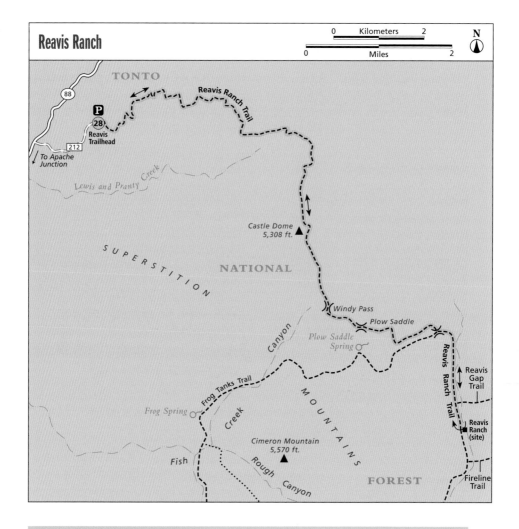

Reavis Ranch

Reavis Ranch Trail

TONTO

88

P
28
Reavis
Trailhead

212

To Apache
Junction

Lewis and Pranty Creek

SUPERSTITION

NATIONAL

Castle Dome
5,308 ft.

Windy Pass

Plow Saddle

Plow Saddle
Spring

Canyon

Frog Tanks Trail

Frog Spring

Creek

MOUNTAINS

Cimeron Mountain
5,570 ft.

Fish

Rough Canyon

Reavis Ranch Trail

Reavis
Gap
Trail

Reavis
Ranch
(site)

FOREST

Fireline
Trail

Kilometers 0 2

Miles 0 2

N

NOTHING LASTS FOREVER

When purchased by the Forest Service in the 1960s, the historic ranch house was still intact and usable as an emergency shelter. Unfortunately, years of weather and vandalism took their toll, and the building was finally burned to the ground by careless campers. Although the ruins of the house were cleaned up and removed, you may find artifacts from the old ranching days—please leave everything as you find it.

Most species of yuccca have long, narrow leaves growing from their base or main stem.

Reavis Ranch Trail now drops into Reavis Valley and turns south along the west side of the valley. Reavis Creek itself is graced with Arizona sycamore as well as scattered ponderosa pine mixed with pinyon pine and juniper. You'll meet the Reavis Gap Trail joining from the left at 10.3 miles. The trail passes the old Reavis apple orchard, then emerges into a meadow next to Reavis Creek. This was the site of the old ranch house. You can usually find flowing water in the creek upstream about 0.7 mile.

Miles and Directions

0.0   Begin at Reavis Trailhead.

5.6   Reach first saddle.

6.9   Cross Windy Pass.

7.8   Cross Plow Saddle.

9.2   Frog Tanks Trail junction; stay on Reavis Ranch Trail.

10.3   Reavis Gap Trail junction; continue south.

10.6   Arrive at Reavis Ranch site.

21.2   Retrace your steps to Reavis Trailhead.

29 Upper Fish Creek

Fish Creek is a major canyon system that drains the north-central portion of the Superstition Mountains. The trails on this loop are rough and see little use, but the upside of your slightly tougher journey is a chance to see some of the least visited country in the Superstition Wilderness. A bonus is a visit to the site of the historic Reavis Ranch. A seasonal stream in lower Rogers Canyon, a tributary of Fish Creek, is yet another delight of this backpack trip.

Start: About 30 miles northeast of Apache Junction

Distance: 33.1-mile loop

Approximate hiking time: 3–4 days

Elevation change: 6,820 feet

Difficulty: Strenuous due to distance, elevation change, and faint trails

Seasons: Fall through spring

Trail surface: Dirt and rocks

Water: Seasonal in Reavis Creek south of the ranch site, in Rogers Canyon and Fish Creek, and at Frog Spring and Plow Saddle Spring

Other trail users: Horses

Land status: Superstition Wilderness, Tonto National Forest

Nearest town: Apache Junction

Fees and permits: Group size limited to 15; stay limit 14 days.

Maps: USGS Pinyon Mountain and Iron Mountain; Trail Illustrated Superstition and Four Peaks Wildernesses; USFS Superstition Wilderness, USFS Tonto National Forest

Trail contact: Mesa Ranger District, Tonto National Forest

Finding the trailhead: From Apache Junction, drive 20 miles east on Highway 88 to the end of the pavement. Continue another 7.4 miles on the gravel road to Reavis Ranch Road (Forest Road 212) and then turn right. Now drive 3.0 miles to the Reavis Trailhead at the end of the road. GPS: N33° 33.38' W111° 15.55'

The Hike

Follow the Reavis Ranch Trail southeast up the complex ridges north of Lewis and Pranty Creek. About a mile east of Plow Saddle, the Frog Tanks Trail goes right into the Fish Creek drainage at an unnamed saddle—this will be our return route on the loop portion of the hike. You'll pass the junction with the Reavis Gap Trail and then enter Reavis Valley, the site of the old ranch. There is usually flowing water in the creek south of the ranch. Continue south on the Reavis Ranch Trail, past the junction with the Fireline Trail, to Reavis Saddle at the head of Reavis Creek. From the saddle, follow the Reavis Ranch Trail as it drops down Grave Canyon into Rogers Canyon.

Turn right and follow the Rogers Canyon Trail down its namesake canyon. This section of the canyon is very rugged and scenic—watch for a huge boulder jammed in a crack high up on the southwest wall. There is usually water in a few pools along the bed. As the canyon swings a bit west, watch for a cliff dwelling in a cave on the

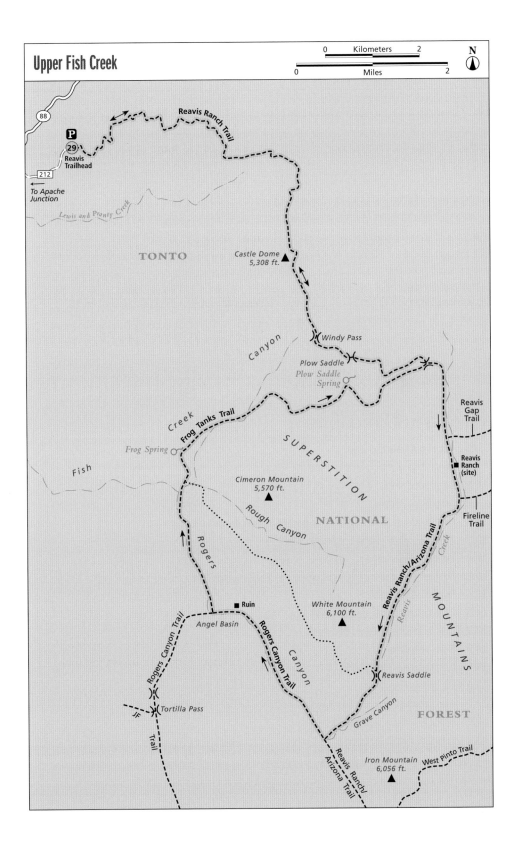

Upper Fish Creek

Kilometers
0   2

Miles
0   2

N

88

P

29
Reavis
Trailhead

212

To Apache
Junction

Lewis and Pranty Creek

TONTO

Reavis Ranch Trail

Castle Dome
5,308 ft.

Windy Pass

Plow Saddle

Plow Saddle
Spring

Canyon

Creek

Frog Tanks Trail

Frog Spring

Fish

SUPERSTITION

Reavis
Gap
Trail

Reavis
Ranch
(site)

Cimeron Mountain
5,570 ft.

Rough Canyon

NATIONAL

Fireline
Trail

Rogers

Reavis Ranch/Arizona Trail

Reavis Creek

MOUNTAINS

Ruin

Angel Basin

Rogers Canyon Trail

Rogers Canyon Trail

White Mountain
6,100 ft.

Canyon

Tortilla Pass

JF

Trail

Reavis Saddle

Grave Canyon

FOREST

Reavis Ranch/
Arizona Trail

Iron Mountain
6,056 ft.

West Pinto Trail

north wall. This well-preserved ruin is a popular destination. There are many such ruins in the Superstitions. Besides cliff dwellings like these, many pit houses remain; there is even a structure thought to be an astronomical observatory. Dating from the Pre-Columbian era, these historic sites are fragile; please don't climb on the walls or otherwise disturb these ancient remains. There is seasonal water in the creek bed below the ruin. You will soon reach Angel Basin; turn right here onto the Frog Tanks Trail and continue down Rogers Canyon to its end at Fish Creek. You should pick up water from one of the seasonal pools in the bed of Rogers Canyon, as there's no reliable water on the remainder of the hike.

Follow the Frog Tanks Trail out of Fish Creek. Frog Spring is marked by an old trough—the unreliable spring is up the drainage above the trough. After passing the old trough, the trail plunges steeply back to the bottom of Fish Creek, then follows it until just past Paradise Canyon. It then climbs the slopes east of Fish Creek and contours to Plow Saddle Spring. The portion of the trail from Fish Creek to the Reavis Ranch Trail is a former jeep trail and is easier going than the section in Rogers Canyon and Fish Creek. Though the trough at Plow Saddle Spring is dry, you may find seasonal water in the ravine bed above and below the trail crossing. After the spring, the trail climbs gradually to end at the Reavis Ranch Trail in an unnamed saddle, completing the loop. Turn left onto the Reavis Ranch Trail to return to the trailhead.

Miles and Directions

0.0 Begin at Reavis Trailhead.

5.6 Reach first saddle.

6.9 Cross Windy Pass.

7.8 Cross Plow Saddle.

9.2 Frog Tanks Trail junction; continue east on Reavis Ranch Trail.

10.3 Reavis Gap Trail junction; continue south.

10.6 Pass Reavis Ranch site.

10.8 Fireline Trail junction; stay right (south) on Reavis Ranch Trail.

13.5 Cross Reavis Saddle.

14.8 Rogers Canyon Trail junction; turn right.

17.3 Frog Tanks Trail junction; turn right.

18.9 Cross Fish Creek.

19.6 Pass seasonal Frog Spring.

20.8 Trail leaves Fish Creek.

22.5 Pass seasonal Plow Saddle Spring.

23.9 Reavis Ranch Trail junction; turn left.

33.1 Return to Reavis Trailhead.

Option

Instead of following the Reavis Ranch, Rogers Canyon, and Frog Tanks Trails down Rogers Canyon, you can leave the Reavis Ranch Trail near Reavis Saddle at the head of Reavis Creek, southeast of White Mountain, for a rugged but rewarding cross-country route across high ridges. You'll need the USGS topographic maps, the USFS wilderness map, and skill in cross-country hiking and route finding to follow this route. Work your way through the chaparral brush toward the ridge south of the summit of White Mountain. It becomes less brushy as you climb onto the ridge. As a side trip, you can easily hike to the summit of White Mountain, which is only 0.1 mile north. Now turn southwest along the ridge to reach the major ridge running northwest to the confluence of Rogers Canyon and Fish Creek. The views along this open, grassy ridge are spectacular. The ridge gradually descends as you follow it above the depths of well-named Rough Canyon. At the end of the ridge, drop west directly to the end of Rogers Canyon, working your way around small cliffs. This route is 3.7 miles shorter than the normal route along the trails, but the cross-country hiking will be slow enough that you won't save much time, if any. You'll also have an additional 800 feet of elevation gain because of the climb over White Mountain.

GREEN TIP

On the trail eat grains and veggies instead of meat, which has a higher energy cost. And pack food in plastic zipper bags that you can reuse to tote garbage out.

30 Pinyon Mountain

This hike is a good introduction to the less-popular eastern portion of the Superstition Wilderness. You'll encounter a wide variety of terrain, from Sonoran Desert to pinyon-juniper forest, as the trail runs along Two Bar Ridge. The loop traverses just below the summit of Pinyon Mountain, one of the highest peaks in the northeastern Superstition Mountains. A side hike to the summit is an easy option.

Start: About 53 miles east of Apache Junction

Distance: 11.0-mile loop

Approximate hiking time: 6–7 hours

Elevation change: 3,340 feet

Difficulty: Strenuous due to distance, elevation change, and faint trails

Seasons: Fall through spring

Trail surface: Dirt and rocks

Water: None

Other trail users: Horses

Land status: Superstition Wilderness, Tonto National Forest

Nearest town: Apache Junction

Fees and permits: Group size limited to 15; stay limit 14 days.

Maps: USGS Pinyon Mountain and Two Bar Ridge; Trail Illustrated Superstition and Four Peaks Wildernesses; USFS Superstition Wilderness, USFS Tonto National Forest

Trail contact: Tonto Basin Ranger District, Tonto National Forest

Finding the trailhead: From Apache Junction, drive 20 miles east on Highway 88 to the end of the pavement. Continue another 20 miles on the gravel road to Roosevelt Dam, then turn right to remain on Highway 88, which is now paved. Continue 8.6 miles, then turn right onto Forest Road 449, the Campaign Creek Road, which is maintained dirt. Go 1.9 miles, turn right at a fork to remain on FR 449, and continue 0.6 mile to the Tule Trailhead. GPS: N33° 35.61' W111° 4.60'

You can also reach FR 449 from Globe by driving about 20 miles west on Highway 88, which is paved.

The Hike

Start on the Tule Canyon Trail, which wanders southwest from the trailhead, working its way through the foothills toward Tule Canyon. After 1.0 mile the trail crosses Tule Canyon, after which it turns more to the west for a while and climbs onto a ridge south of Tule Canyon. Then it abruptly turns south and climbs steeply to the top of a ridge north of Two Bar Canyon. Now follow the trail west along the ridge. The Tule Canyon Trail ends on the top of Two Bar Ridge. Turn right here and follow the Two Bar Ridge Trail north toward the rounded bulk of Pinyon Mountain.

Notice that you left the saguaro cactus of the Sonoran Desert behind as you climbed. The grassy top of Two Bar Ridge has scattered pinyon pine and juniper. The trail wanders north, then west, and north again as it follows the twists and turns of the ridge. Finally, it climbs partway up Pinyon Mountain, then contours around the southeast slopes of the peak before descending northeast to end at Forest Road 83.

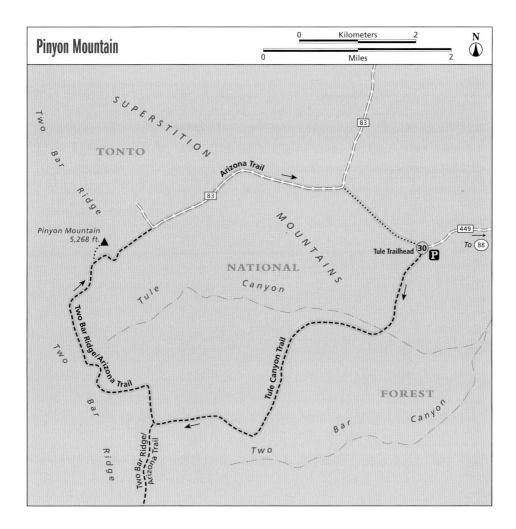

Turn right and follow the road as it drops off the ridge, then turns north into a drainage system. After leaving the drainage, it climbs over a low pass to the east. As you emerge from the mountains onto the gently sloping desert plain, the road turns north. Leave the road at this point and hike cross-country about 1.1 miles to the Tule Trailhead and your vehicle.

Miles and Directions

0.0 Begin at Tule Trailhead.

1.0 Cross Tule Canyon.

4.3 Two Bar Ridge Trail junction; turn right.

6.4 Trail ascends toward Pinyon Mountain.

7.7 Junction Forest Road 83; turn right.

9.9 Leave the road and hike cross-country southeast.

11.0 Return to Tule Trailhead.

Option

You can easily climb Pinyon Mountain for some great views. Leave the trail where it starts to contour below the summit and hike cross-country about 0.2 mile north to the rounded summit. This option adds 0.4 mile and less than 300 feet of climbing to the hike.

SHORT FORESTS

Juniper and pinyon pine commonly occur together in the mountains of central Arizona and combine to create a pigmy forest about 10 to 20 feet high. The several species of juniper are slow-growing, drought-resistant trees, and they appear first as you gain elevation. Pinyon pine need a little more water and gradually mix with juniper as you climb. These shaggy pine trees are taller than juniper and have short needles. The pinecones produce a tasty nut that was long a staple food for Native Americans. Occasionally pinyon pine grow to 40 feet and often provide a soft bed of needles and an inviting patch of shade around their bases. They also produce a lot of sticky sap, which runs down the trunk and drips from the branches.

31 Fireline Loop

The classic eastern Superstition Wilderness loop hike, the Fireline Loop takes you through the highest portion of the Superstition Wilderness. Stands of ponderosa pine grow along this route, which surprises many hikers who are only familiar with the more accessible, and much lower elevation, western Superstition Mountains. You'll have a chance to climb 6,266-foot Mound Mountain, the highest peak in the range, and visit the site of the historic Reavis Ranch. A long section of the loop follows Campaign Creek, one of the most beautiful of Superstition Wilderness canyons.

Start: About 54 miles east of Apache Junction

Distance: 14.5-mile loop

Approximate hiking time: 2 days

Elevation change: 3,380 feet

Difficulty: Strenuous due to distance and elevation change

Seasons: Fall and spring

Trail surface: Dirt and rocks

Water: Campaign Creek near the trailhead, Walnut Spring, seasonal Pine Creek and Reavis Creek, Whiskey Spring, Black Jack Spring, Brushy Spring, seasonal upper Campaign Creek

Other trail users: Horses

Land status: Superstition Wilderness, Tonto National Forest

Nearest town: Apache Junction

Fees and permits: Group size limited to 15; stay limit 14 days.

Maps: USGS Pinyon Mountain, Two Bar Mountain, Haunted Canyon, and Iron Mountain; Trail Illustrated Superstition and Four Peaks Wildernesses; USFS Superstition Wilderness, USFS Tonto National Forest

Trail contact: Tonto Basin Ranger District, Tonto National Forest

Finding the trailhead: From Apache Junction, drive 20 miles east on Highway 88 to the end of the pavement. Continue another 20 miles on the gravel road to Roosevelt Dam, then turn right to remain on Highway 88, which is now paved. Continue 8.6 miles, then turn right onto Forest Road 449, the Campaign Creek Road, which is maintained dirt. Go 1.9 miles, then turn left at a fork onto Forest Road 449A and continue 5.2 miles to the end of the road at the Reavis Mountain School. FR 449A follows Campaign Creek and crosses it numerous times. This route requires a high-clearance vehicle and may be washed out and impassable after major storms. The trailhead is on private land—please park in the signed trailhead parking. There is no camping at the trailhead. GPS: N33° 31.83' W111° 4.84'

You can also reach FR 449A from Globe by driving about 20 miles west on Highway 88, which is paved.

The Hike

After leaving the Campaign Trailhead on the Campaign Creek Trail, hike through the Reavis Mountain School (there are several buildings and tent camps—please respect private property and stay on the trail) and continue southwest along Campaign Creek. This section of the creek has a permanent flow of water from several nearby springs. Just after a side canyon comes in from the right, turn right onto the Reavis Gap Trail. This trail is not shown on the USGS maps, and sections can be difficult to follow. First climb over a low ridge, then head west up an unnamed canyon system, climbing steadily. After you cross the normally dry wash, the grade steepens as the trail heads for Reavis Gap, a saddle on Two Bar Ridge. Just after passing through Reavis Gap, the Two Bar Ridge Trail branches right. (Walnut Spring is about 0.5 mile north on the Two Bar Ridge Trail.) Stay on the Reavis Gap Trail as it passes through another saddle, then swings south and drops into Pine Creek. There is seasonal water in Pine Creek.

After crossing Pine Creek, head southwest and climb gradually toward another saddle. The trail then drops gradually west down a tributary of Reavis Creek and ends at the Reavis Ranch Trail on the west side of Reavis Creek. Turn left and hike a short distance upstream to the historic ranch site. There is usually water in the creek south of the ranch site. (See Reavis Ranch hike description for more information.)

Continue the hike by heading south on the Reavis Ranch Trail. Turn left (east) onto the Fireline Trail before reaching the first major drainage entering on the left. Parts of this trail follow an old bulldozer track made by the USDA Forest Service while fighting a forest fire in 1966. Wildfires are common in this remote country, and difficult to fight. In the early days of this wilderness, it was thought that all wildfires should be aggressively suppressed, and bulldozers were used to build access roads and construct fire lines, leaving prominent scars. The Forest Service now recognizes that lightning-caused fires are part of the natural forest cycle and are necessary to keep the wilderness wild. Such natural fires are allowed to burn uncontrolled, except for monitoring and containment efforts to keep the fire from threatening developed areas outside the wilderness. Another fire burned the area in the 1980s, but because low-impact firefighting techniques were used, there was much less impact to the landscape.

You'll mostly be in a mixed chaparral brush and pinyon-juniper forest along the first part of the Fireline Trail. After passing Whiskey Spring, the trail turns more to the northeast and climbs up a drainage to the divide between Reavis Creek and Pine Creek. Now it heads southeast and descends gradually into the head of Pine Creek. Pockets of tall ponderosa pine grow in favored locations here—hence the name of the creek. The old bulldozer trail suddenly turns northeast, drops steeply into the bed of Pine Creek, and follows the drainage for a short distance before climbing out to the east and crossing the divide between Pine and Campaign Creeks. Now it plunges steeply into Campaign Creek, passing Black Jack Spring just before ending at the Pinto Peak Trail in Campaign Creek.

Now turn left again and follow the Pinto Peak Trail down Campaign Creek. After the rugged country you've just crossed, it's a joy to wander down the scenic canyon

A backpacker descends the Fireline Trail toward Reavis Creek. ▶

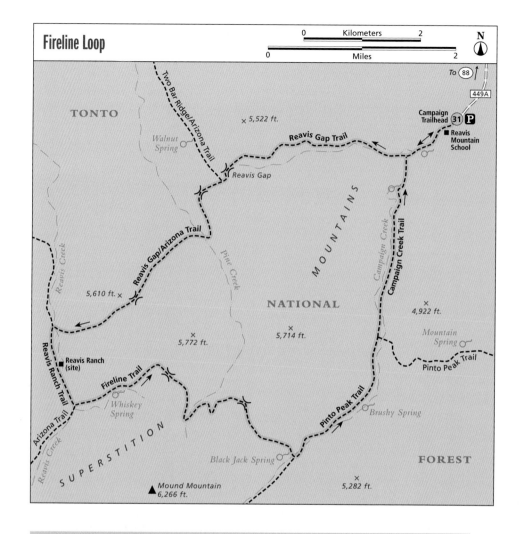

Fireline Loop

FIRE SURVIVORS

The high country of the eastern Superstitions is frequently burned by wildfires. You might wonder how any pine trees manage to grow here. Ponderosa pine are actually well adapted to fire. The thick, platy bark of mature trees insulates the living cambium from the heat of a fire. As long as the fire is not so hot that it jumps into the crowns of the trees, most ponderosa pine survive a wildfire. Frequent fires keep underbrush and dead wood from accumulating, and lower the average intensity of fires.

bottom. There's seasonal water in the creek bed. The Pinto Peak Trail veers right and climbs out of Campaign Creek at the junction with the Campaign Creek Trail. Go left here onto the Campaign Creek Trail and continue north down Campaign Creek. Finally, the trail climbs over a low saddle to avoid a narrow, rough section of the canyon bottom, then meets the Reavis Gap Trail. Stay right to return to the Campaign Trailhead.

Miles and Directions

0.0   Campaign Trailhead.

0.7   Junction Reavis Gap Trail; turn right.

2.9   Reavis Gap/Two Bar Ridge Trail junction; stay left.

3.7   Cross Pine Creek.

5.7   Reavis Ranch Trail junction; turn left.

6.1   Pass Reavis Ranch site.

6.5   Fireline Trail junction; turn left.

7.6   Arrive at Reavis Creek–Pine Creek divide.

9.9   Pinto Peak Trail junction; turn left.

11.7   Campaign Creek Trail junction; turn left.

13.8   Reavis Gap Trail junction; turn right.

14.5   Campaign Trailhead.

Options

Option 1. At Reavis Gap, turn right onto the Two Bar Ridge Trail and hike 1.2 miles north, past Walnut Spring, to the point where the trail starts to drop into a tributary of Pine Creek. This point is a fine overlook of lower Pine Creek and Two Bar Ridge. This option adds 2.4 miles and 200 feet of elevation change to the hike.

Option 2. Where the Reavis Gap Trail crosses Pine Creek, turn left and hike cross-country up Pine Creek to the Fireline Trail. Sections of upper Pine Creek are rough and slow because of large boulders and dense brush. It's 1.8 miles to the Fireline Trail, and you'll climb about 620 feet. This option shortens the loop by 5.6 miles, but is much more difficult than staying on the trails.

Option 3. When the Fireline Trail starts down into Pine Creek, leave the trail and hike cross-country south along the pinyon and juniper–covered ridge. Though the upper part of this ridge is brushy, with some route finding you can make a reasonably brush-free ascent to the top of Mound Mountain. At 6,266 feet, this round summit is the highest point in the Superstition Mountains and has an appropriately commanding view of the range. This option adds 2.6 miles and 800 feet of elevation change to the trip.

Option 4. At the junction of the Fireline Trail and Pinto Peak Trail, turn right and hike up the Pinto Peak Trail to the saddle at the head of Campaign Creek. You'll get good views of upper Pinto Creek and the rugged country around Iron Mountain and Pinto Peak in the southeast corner of the Superstition Mountains. This hike adds 3.2 miles to the trip and 690 feet of elevation gain.

32 Mountain Spring

For those who wish to hike up gorgeous Campaign Creek without having to do a backpack trip, this moderate day hike takes you up the most scenic lower portion of the creek within the Superstition Wilderness. A permanent stream graces the first part of the trail up Campaign Creek, and the goal for the hike is the appropriately named Mountain Spring at the eastern edge of the Superstition Mountains.

Start: About 54 miles east of Apache Junction

Distance: 7.8 miles out and back

Approximate hiking time: 5 hours

Elevation change: 1,210 feet

Difficulty: Moderate due to distance and elevation change

Seasons: Fall and spring

Trail surface: Dirt and rocks

Water: Campaign Creek near the trailhead, seasonally at Mountain Spring

Other trail users: Horses

Land status: Superstition Wilderness, Tonto National Forest

Nearest town: Apache Junction

Fees and permits: Group size limited to 15 people; stay limit 14 days.

Maps: USGS Two Bar Mountain and Haunted Canyon; Trail Illustrated Superstition and Four Peaks Wildernesses; USFS Superstition Wilderness, USFS Tonto National Forest

Trail contact: Tonto Basin Ranger District, Tonto National Forest

Finding the trailhead: From Apache Junction, drive 20 miles east on Highway 88 to the end of the pavement. Continue another 20 miles on the gravel road to Roosevelt Dam, then turn right to remain on paved Highway 88. Continue 8.6 miles, then turn right onto Forest Road 449A, the Campaign Creek Road, which is maintained dirt. Go 1.9 miles, then turn left at a fork onto Forest Road 449A and continue 5.2 miles to the end of the road at the Reavis Mountain School. FR 449A follows Campaign Creek and crosses it numerous times. This route requires a high-clearance vehicle and may be washed out and impassable after major storms. The trailhead is on private land—please park in the signed trailhead parking. No camping is permitted at the trailhead. GPS: N33° 31.83' W111° 4.84'

You can also reach FR 449 from Globe by driving about 20 miles west on paved Highway 88.

The Hike

After leaving the Campaign Trailhead on the Campaign Creek Trail, hike through the Reavis Mountain School (there are several buildings and tent camps—please respect private property and stay on the trail) and continue southwest along Campaign Creek. The lower section of the creek has a delightful, permanent flow of water. At 0.7 mile you pass the junction with the Reavis Gap Trail; stay left on the Campaign Creek Trail as it climbs over a saddle to avoid a rough section of the canyon bottom. Continue south on the trail as the canyon climbs gradually. At the Pinto Peak Trail junction, turn left and follow this little-used trail over a low saddle on the ridge east

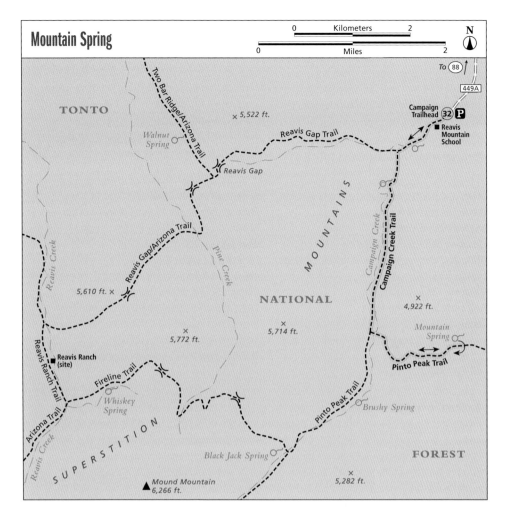

Mountain Spring

0   Kilometers   2

0   Miles   2

N

TONTO

Two Bar Ridge/Arizona Trail

Walnut Spring

× 5,522 ft.

Reavis Gap Trail

Reavis Gap

Reavis Gap/Arizona Trail

Pine Creek

Reavis Creek

5,610 ft. ×

NATIONAL

5,772 ft. ×

5,714 ft. ×

MOUNTAINS

Campaign Creek

Campaign Creek Trail

4,922 ft. ×

Mountain Spring

Pinto Peak Trail

To 88

449A

Campaign Trailhead 32 P

Reavis Mountain School

Reavis Ranch (site)

Reavis Ranch Trail

Fireline Trail

Whiskey Spring

Arizona Trail

Reavis Creek

SUPERSTITION

Black Jack Spring

Mound Mountain 6,266 ft.

Pinto Peak Trail

Brushy Spring

5,282 ft. ×

FOREST

of Campaign Creek. Now the trail starts down into the head of a drainage and soon reaches Mountain Spring.

Miles and Directions

0.0 Begin at Campaign Trailhead.

0.7 Reavis Gap Trail junction; stay left.

2.8 Pinto Peak Trail junction; turn left.

3.9 Arrive at Mountain Spring.

7.8 Return to trailhead.

Options

Continue on the Pinto Peak Trail to its end at Forest Road 306. This adds 2.5 miles and 530 feet of elevation change to the hike. You can also turn right onto the Pinto Peak Trail and explore up Campaign Creek as far as you like.

33 Reavis Creek

A fine backpack trip in the eastern Superstition Wilderness, this hike is a scenic loop around Iron and Mound Mountains through the highest portion of the Superstition Mountains. You'll encounter stands of tall ponderosa pine, seasonal creeks, and several springs. The loop also traverses the headwaters of Campaign Creek and West Pinto Creek, two of the least visited areas of the wilderness.

Start: About 42 miles east of Apache Junction

Distance: 18.1-mile loop

Approximate hiking time: 2–3 days

Elevation change: 5,740 feet

Difficulty: Strenuous due to distance, elevation change, and little-used trails

Seasons: Fall through spring

Trail surface: Dirt and rocks

Water: Seasonal at Rogers Spring, Iron Mountain Spring, and Crockett Spring; year-round in Reavis Creek, Campaign Creek, and West Fork of Pinto Creek

Other trail users: Horses

Land status: Superstition Wilderness, Tonto National Forest

Nearest town: Apache Junction

Fees and permits: Group size limited to 15; stay limit 14 days.

Maps: USGS Iron Mountain and Haunted Canyon; Trail Illustrated Superstition and Four Peaks Wildernesses; USFS Superstition Wilderness, USFS Tonto National Forest

Trail contact: Mesa Ranger District, Tonto National Forest

Finding the trailhead: From Apache Junction, go about 18 miles east on U.S. Highway 60, then turn left onto Queen Creek Road. Follow this paved road 1.9 miles, then turn right onto Forest Road 357, a maintained dirt road. Continue 3.1 miles to the junction with Forest Road 172, then turn left. Go 12.5 miles on this maintained dirt road, then turn right onto Forest Road 172A. After 3.6 miles, turn left at the junction with Forest Road 650 and continue 0.4 mile to the Rogers Trough Trailhead. This last section of FR 172A is rough and may require a high-clearance vehicle. GPS: N33° 25.35' W111° 10.41'

The Hike

Start by following the Reavis Ranch Trail down Rogers Canyon, heading northwest from the trailhead. Watch for Grave Canyon on the right, and make sure you follow the Reavis Ranch Trail (northeast up this side canyon). The Rogers Canyon Trail forks left and continues down the main canyon. The Reavis Ranch Trail climbs steeply to the Reavis Saddle on the ridge northwest of Iron Mountain. Chaparral brush and pinyon-juniper forest are the dominant vegetation, but some nice groves of ponderosa pine also grow along the valley floor.

The Reavis Ranch Trail continues to descend gradually down Reavis Creek. Turn right onto the Fireline Trail (the site of the Reavis Ranch is 0.3 mile farther up the Reavis Ranch Trail, and there's usually water in the creek just above the ranch site). The trail climbs past Whiskey Spring, then over the saddle between Reavis and Pine

Ponderosa pines flourish in the cool microclimate along the upper reaches of Reavis Creek.

Creeks. It drops into Pine Creek, then climbs over another saddle on the divide between Pine and Campaign Creeks. A steep descent takes you past Black Jack Spring and into Campaign Creek.

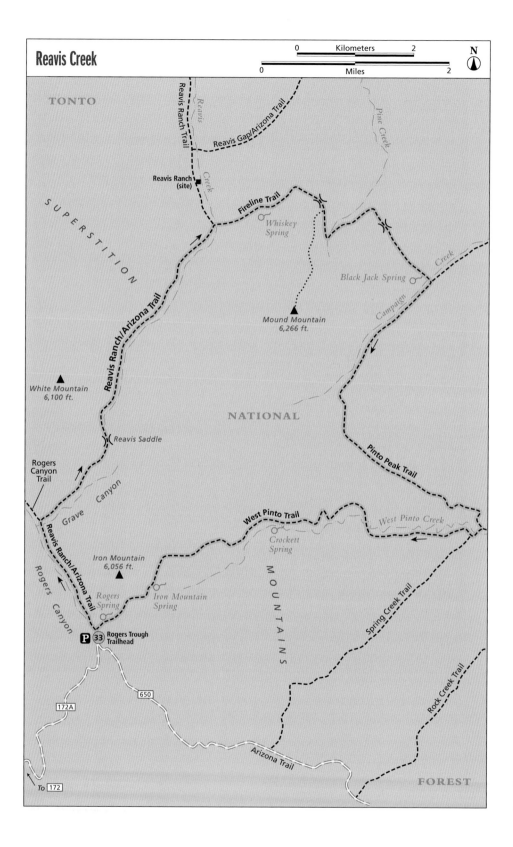

Reavis Creek

CHAPARRAL CHALLENGE

Chaparral is common at intermediate elevations in Arizona. It's a community of shrubs rather than a single plant. Common members are manzanita, which is easily recognized by its brittle, red-barked branches and small, oval green leaves; mountain mahogany, which has smaller, ridged leaves; and scrub oak, which is a tough, low-growing evergreen oak. Really thick stands of chaparral can reach as high as 10 feet and are very difficult to force your way through. Most stands are lower and have open lanes, often made by deer and other animals, that allow you to find a route. Though a pain for hikers, chaparral is valuable cover for a number of animals and birds. It burns furiously after a drought but grows back rapidly from the roots, which survive the fire's heat.

Continue by turning right onto the Pinto Peak Trail and hiking up Campaign Creek to the pass at its head. Now the trail drops southeast down a ridge system into the Pinto Creek drainage, meeting the West Fork of Pinto Creek at Oak Flat. Turn right here, onto the West Pinto Trail, and hike west up the creek. The trail climbs along the slopes south of the creek for about a mile, then crosses the creek bed to the north side where it continues for another mile before descending back to the creek bed and meeting Crockett Spring. (Crockett Spring is shown correctly on the Superstition Wilderness map, but incorrectly on the Iron Mountain USGS map.) After staying in or near the creek for less than a mile, the trail leaves the bed and climbs a ridge toward Iron Mountain. It swings south to Iron Mountain Spring, then climbs over a pass on the shoulder of Iron Mountain. Finally, the trail descends past Rogers Spring and ends at the Rogers Trough Trailhead.

Miles and Directions

0.0   Begin at Rogers Trough Trailhead.
1.4   Grave Canyon; turn right.
2.6   Cross Reavis Saddle.
5.3   Fireline Trail junction; turn right.
6.4   Cross saddle between Reavis and Pine Creeks.
8.6   Pinto Peak Trail junction; turn right.
11.2 Reach pass at head of Campaign Creek.
12.6 Oak Flat/West Pinto Trail junction; turn right.
15.3 Arrive at Crockett Spring (unsigned).
17.4 Cross pass on shoulder of Iron Mountain.
18.1 Return to Rogers Trough Trailhead.

34 Angel Basin

This backpack trip has it all—scenic canyons, views from high ridges, seasonal creeks, and a well-preserved pre-Columbian ruin. Upper Rogers Canyon is one of the gems of the Superstition Wilderness, and Angel Basin is a surprising open valley in a country of deep canyons and rugged peaks. The route also crosses one of the highest passes in the Superstition Mountains, providing views of much of the range.

Start: About 37 miles east of Apache Junction
Distance: 12.0-mile loop
Approximate hiking time: 8 hours or 2 days
Elevation change: 2,940 feet
Difficulty: Strenuous due to distance and elevation change
Seasons: Fall through spring
Trail surface: Dirt and rocks
Water: Seasonal along Rogers Canyon
Other trail users: Horses

Land status: Superstition Wilderness, Tonto National Forest
Nearest town: Apache Junction
Fees and permits: Group size limited to 15; stay limit 14 days.
Maps: USGS Iron Mountain; Trail Illustrated Superstition and Four Peaks Wildernesses; USFS Superstition Wilderness, USFS Tonto National Forest
Trail contact: Globe and Mesa Ranger Districts, Tonto National Forest

Finding the trailhead: From Apache Junction, go about 18 miles east on U.S. Highway 60, then turn left onto Queen Creek Road. Follow this paved road 1.9 miles, then turn right onto Forest Road 357, a maintained dirt road. Continue 3.1 miles to the junction with Forest Road 172, then turn left. Go 12.5 miles on this maintained dirt road, then go left onto Forest Road 172B. Continue 1.5 miles to a locked gate, then turn right and park at the Woodbury Trailhead. This road is passable to ordinary vehicles except after a major storm. GPS: N33° 24.85 W111° 12.36'

The Hike

Hike north on the JF Trail, then turn right onto the Woodbury Trail, an old mining road. (The JF Trail will be our return route.) Follow the Woodbury Trail as it climbs steeply east to meet Forest Road 172A, Rogers Trough Road, then follow the road to the Rogers Trough Trailhead. The hike takes you down Rogers Canyon on the Reavis Ranch Trail. You'll pass the West Pinto Trail just after leaving the trailhead; continue on the Reavis Ranch Trail. Turn left where the Reavis Ranch Trail veers right up Grave Canyon, and follow the Rogers Canyon Trail northwest down Rogers Canyon to Angel Basin. (See the Upper Fish Creek hike description for more information on this section.)

Hiking up Rogers Canyon, if you can take your eyes off the ▶
view, enjoy the large variety of vegetation, especially after a rain.

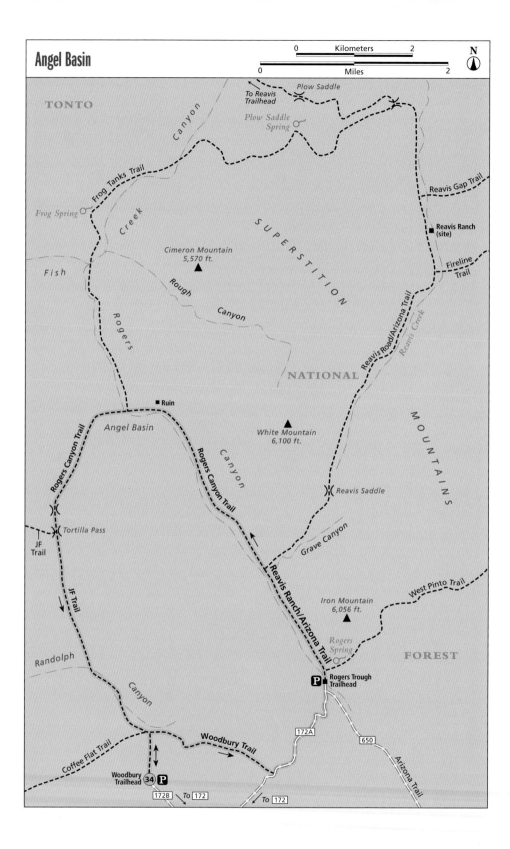

Angel Basin

0 — Kilometers — 2
0 — Miles — 2

N

TONTO

To Reavis Trailhead

Plow Saddle

Plow Saddle Spring

Frog Tanks Trail

Frog Spring

Creek

SUPERSTITION

Reavis Gap Trail

Reavis Ranch (site)

Cimeron Mountain 5,570 ft.

Fireline Trail

Fish

Rough Canyon

Rogers

Reavis Road/Arizona Trail

Reavis Creek

NATIONAL

Ruin

Angel Basin

Rogers Canyon Trail

Canyon

White Mountain 6,100 ft.

MOUNTAINS

Rogers Canyon Trail

Tortilla Pass

Reavis Saddle

JF Trail

Reavis Ranch/Arizona Trail

Grave Canyon

JF Trail

West Pinto Trail

Iron Mountain 6,056 ft.

Randolph

Rogers Spring

FOREST

Canyon

Rogers Trough Trailhead

P

Coffee Flat Trail

Woodbury Trail

172A

650

Woodbury Trailhead

34

P

Arizona Trail

172B

To 172

To 172

From Angel Basin, follow the Rogers Canyon Trail as it leaves Rogers Canyon (the Frog Tanks Trail continues down the canyon) and heads west and then south up an unnamed tributary canyon. A steady climb leads to Tortilla Pass and the junction with the JF Trail. Turn left onto the JF Trail and start a steep descent down a tributary of Randolph Canyon. At the bottom of this long descent, cross the Woodbury Trail and continue south to the trailhead.

Miles and Directions

0.0   Begin at Woodbury Trailhead.

0.5   Woodbury Trail junction; turn right.

2.1   FR 172A junction; turn left.

3.4   FR 650 junction; turn left.

3.6   Reach Rogers Trough Trailhead and start down Rogers Canyon on Reavis Ranch Trail.

4.9   Reavis Ranch Trail goes right up Grave Canyon; turn left onto Rogers Canyon Trail.

7.4   Angel Basin and junction with Frog Tanks Trail; turn left and remain on Rogers Canyon Trail.

9.0   Tortilla Pass/JF Trail junction; turn left onto JF Trail.

11.5   Cross Woodbury Trail; take JF Trail right (south).

12.0   Return to Woodbury Trailhead.

Option

If you have two vehicles, you can leave a vehicle at the Woodbury Trailhead and start the hike from the Rogers Trough Trailhead (see the Reavis Creek hike for trailhead directions). This avoids the 2.9-mile climb on the Woodbury Trail and Rogers Trough Road at the start of the hike.

35 Randolph Canyon

This hike first descends cross-country through scenic Randolph Canyon, a less-visited canyon in the southern Superstition Mountains, and then returns via the trail up Fraser Canyon. You'll pass JF Ranch, a historic working cattle ranch on the south edge of the Superstition Wilderness.

Start: About 37 miles east of Apache Junction
Distance: 9.1-mile loop
Approximate hiking time: 6 hours
Elevation change: 1,420 feet
Difficulty: Moderate due to distance, elevation change, and cross-country hiking
Seasons: Fall through spring
Trail surface: Dirt and rocks
Water: Randolph Canyon, Dripping Spring
Other trail users: Horses

Land status: Superstition Wilderness, Tonto National Forest
Nearest town: Apache Junction
Fees and permits: Group size limited to 15; stay limit 14 days.
Maps: USGS Weavers Needle and Iron Mountain; Trail Illustrated Superstition and Four Peaks Wildernesses; USFS Superstition Wilderness, USFS Tonto National Forest
Trail contact: Mesa Ranger District, Tonto National Forest

Finding the trailhead: From Apache Junction, go about 18 miles east on U.S. Highway 60, then turn left onto Queen Creek Road. Follow this paved road 1.9 miles, then turn right onto Forest Road 357, a maintained dirt road. Continue 3.1 miles to the junction with Forest Road 172, then turn left. Go 12.5 miles on this maintained dirt road, then go left onto Forest Road 172B. Continue 1.5 miles to a locked gate, then turn right and park at the Woodbury Trailhead. This road is passable to ordinary vehicles except after a major storm. GPS: N33° 24.85 W111° 12.36'

The Hike

Hike north on the JF Trail past the junction with the Coffee Flat and Woodbury Trails—the Coffee Flat Trail will be our return. The JF Trail follows Randolph Canyon downstream to the northwest, then leaves the canyon to climb north. Turn left here, leave the JF Trail, and follow Randolph Canyon cross-country downstream to the west. The going is easy down the wash, and at first the canyon is broad and open, but it narrows somewhat as it turns southwest. You should find seasonal water in the bed, near where the Superstition Wilderness map shows Randolph Spring. Just before Red Tanks Canyon comes in from the right, the Red Tanks Trail drops over a low ridge into Randolph Canyon. Follow the Red Tanks Trail downstream to Fraser Canyon. Dripping Spring, at this junction, normally has water. Turn left onto the Coffee Flat Trail and follow it up Fraser Canyon. About a mile up the canyon you'll pass

Backpackers follow the JF Trail, on the Randolph Canyon loop. ▶

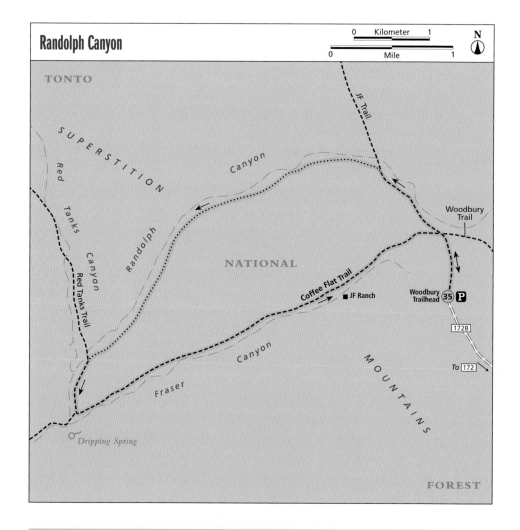

Randolph Canyon

TONTO

SUPERSTITION

Red Tanks Canyon

Red Tanks Trail

Randolph

Canyon

NATIONAL

Canyon

JF Trail

Woodbury Trail

Coffee Flat Trail

■ JF Ranch

Woodbury Trailhead 35 P

172B

MOUNTAINS

To 172

Fraser Canyon

Dripping Spring

FOREST

0   Kilometer   1

0   Mile   1

N

TAMARISK MAKES ITSELF AT HOME

Along Randolph and Fraser Canyons, you'll see tamarisk, a tall, slender shrub with leaves that resemble those of the common juniper. Also known as salt cedar, tamarisk is a native of Middle Eastern deserts but was imported into California as an ornamental and to control erosion. It soon got out of control and has since spread throughout the Colorado River basin, which includes both the Superstition and Mazatzal Mountains. It grows along any stream course with enough underground water to support it. It competes aggressively with native streamside vegetation and often grows so thick it's difficult to hike through. In the fall, the feathery branches turn bright gold, and in the spring and early summer, the plant is a mass of tiny pink flowers.

through a narrower section, then the canyon opens up. After passing the JF Ranch, which is a historic ranch that is still active, you meet the JF Trail junction, completing the loop. Turn right to return to the Woodbury Trailhead.

Miles and Directions

0.0 Begin at Woodbury Trailhead.

0.5 Woodbury and Coffee Flat Trail junction; continue on JF Trail.

1.4 Turn left and hike cross-country down Randolph Canyon.

4.6 Red Tanks Trail junction; turn left.

5.1 Coffee Flat Trail junction; turn left.

8.6 JF Trail junction; turn right.

9.1 Return to Woodbury Trailhead.

36 Coffee Flat Mountain Loop

Starting from the easily accessible Peralta Trailhead, this backpack trip loops around rugged Coffee Flat Mountain. It passes the many-pinnacled summit of Miners Needle and climbs up scenic Red Tanks Canyon. It crosses Red Tanks Divide, one of the most remote passes in the Superstition Mountains, then descends through Upper La Barge Box, a narrow portion of La Barge Canyon.

Start: About 17 miles east of Apache Junction
Distance: 16.9-mile loop
Approximate hiking time: 2 days
Elevation change: 3,090 feet
Difficulty: Strenuous due to distance, elevation change, and faint trails
Seasons: Fall through spring
Trail surface: Dirt and rocks
Water: Dripping Spring, lower Red Tanks Canyon, Upper La Barge Box, Whiskey Spring
Other trail users: Horses

Land status: Superstition Wilderness, Tonto National Forest
Nearest town: Apache Junction
Fees and permits: Group size limited to 15; stay limit 14 days.
Maps: USGS Weavers Needle; Trail Illustrated Superstition and Four Peaks Wildernesses; USFS Superstition Wilderness, USFS Tonto National Forest
Trail contact: Mesa Ranger District, Tonto National Forest

Finding the trailhead: From Apache Junction, drive about 8.5 miles east on U.S. Highway 60, then turn left onto Peralta Road (Forest Road 77), which is maintained dirt. Continue 8 miles to the end of the road at the Peralta Trailhead. GPS: N111° 23.83' W111° 20.89'

The Hike

Start on the Dutchmans Trail and hike east over a low pass. The broad, well-traveled trail continues east along the saguaro cactus–studded foothills at the north edge of Barkley Basin, and heads for the base of Miners Needle, a collection of stone towers visible ahead. Just before the trail starts to switchback up the canyon southeast of Miners Needle, turn right onto the Coffee Flat Trail (the Dutchmans Trail will be our return). This trail heads southeast, then climbs over a low pass into Coffee Flat. It follows the Whitlow Canyon drainage for a short distance downstream to the south, then veers east and climbs across low hills, dropping into a tributary of Randolph Canyon at Reeds Water, the site of an old windmill. The trail heads south for a short distance, then turns east up Randolph Canyon. When Fraser Canyon enters from the north, turn left and follow the Red Tanks Trail up Fraser Canyon. There is usually water at Dripping Spring at this junction.

This aerial view of the western Superstition Mountains ▶
reveals the rugged wilderness.

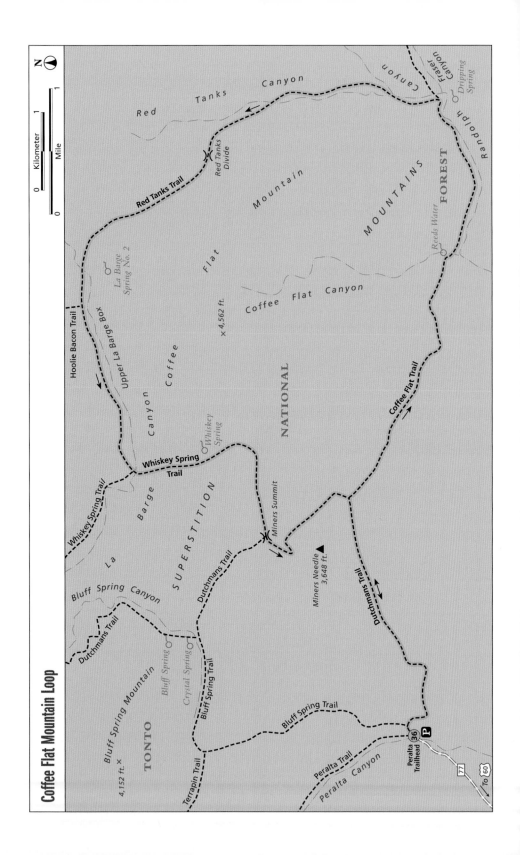

Coffee Flat Mountain Loop

N

0   Kilometer   1

0   Mile   1

Red Tanks Canyon

Fraser Canyon

Dripping Spring

Randolph Canyon

Red Tanks Trail

Red Tanks Divide

Hoolie Bacon Trail

Mountain

MOUNTAINS

FOREST

Reeds Water

La Barge Spring No. 2

Upper La Barge Box

Flat

× 4,562 ft.

Coffee Flat Canyon

Coffee Canyon

NATIONAL

Coffee Flat Trail

Whiskey Spring

Whiskey Spring Trail

Miners Summit

Whiskey Spring Trail

La Barge

SUPERSTITION

Dutchmans Trail

Miners Needle
3,648 ft.

Dutchmans Trail

Bluff Spring Canyon

Dutchmans Trail

Bluff Spring

Crystal Spring

Bluff Spring Trail

TONTO

Bluff Spring Mountain
4,152 ft. ×

Terrapin Trail

Bluff Spring Trail

Peralta Trail

Peralta Canyon

Peralta Trailhead

36

P

77

To 60

SUPERSTITION'S ROCKS: EAST VS. WEST

Two of the common volcanic rock types found throughout the western Superstitions are tuff and rhyolite. Tuff is a yellowish, soft rock that formed from ash spewed from ancient volcanoes. Rhyolite is a somewhat harder gray rock that forms from ash flows. Both rhyolite and tuff cooled from the molten state very quickly, so the mineral crystals that formed the rock had little time to grow. In contrast, the granitic rocks found in the eastern Superstitions formed deep underground, where cooling took place very slowly, allowing time for the crystals to grow.

Watch for Red Tanks Canyon, which enters Fraser Canyon on the left. There is usually water here. Follow the trail a short distance past Red Tanks Canyon, where it veers left and climbs out of Fraser Canyon, crosses a low ridge, then drops into Red Tanks Canyon itself. The trail heads north up the canyon, then climbs west over Red Tanks Divide. This section of the trail is faint in places. At the pass you have great views of the imposing Coffee Flat Mountain to the south. The trail continues northwest down the slopes into La Barge Canyon. You pass the junction with the Hoolie Bacon Trail, and then turn more to the west as the Red Tanks Trail enters Upper La Barge Box. There is seasonal water where the trail crosses the bed.

Turn left onto Whiskey Spring Trail, a well-defined, popular trail that heads south up a tributary of La Barge Canyon. Whiskey Spring is in the bed below the trail. After passing the spring, the trail turns west and climbs over Miners Summit, then drops down to meet the Dutchmans Trail. Turn left onto this heavily used, popular trail and continue past Miners Needle. The trail descends a couple of switchbacks southeast of Miners Needle, then meets the Coffee Flat Trail, completing the loop. Stay right on the Dutchmans Trail to return to the trailhead.

Miles and Directions

0.0 Begin at Peralta Trailhead.
2.4 Coffee Flat Trail junction; turn right.
6.2 Red Tanks Trail junction; turn left.
8.9 Cross Red Tanks Divide.
10.3 Hoolie Bacon Trail junction; continue left.
11.7 Whiskey Spring Trail junction; turn left.
13.4 Dutchmans Trail junction at Miners Summit; turn left.
14.5 Coffee Flat Trail junction; stay right.
16.9 Return to Peralta Trailhead.

37 Bluff Spring Loop

This loop day hike follows good trails though the southwestern Superstition Mountains. The many-pinnacled summit of Miners Needle and the cliffs of Bluff Spring Mountain are special treats on this enjoyable and scenic hike in the Superstition Wilderness.

Start: About 17 miles southeast of Apache Junction

Distance: 7.7-mile loop

Approximate hiking time: 4–5 hours

Elevation change: 1,570 feet

Difficulty: Moderate due to length and elevation change

Seasons: Fall through spring

Trail surface: Dirt and rocks

Water: Bluff Spring

Other trail users: Horses

Land status: Superstition Wilderness, Tonto National Forest

Nearest town: Apache Junction

Fees and permits: Group size limited to 15; stay limit 14 days.

Maps: USGS Weavers Needle; Trail Illustrated Superstition and Four Peaks Wildernesses; USFS Superstition Wilderness, USFS Tonto National Forest

Trail contact: Mesa Ranger District, Tonto National Forest

Finding the trailhead: From Apache Junction, drive about 8.5 miles east on U.S. Highway 60, then turn left onto Peralta Road (Forest Road 77), which is maintained dirt. Continue 8 miles to the end of the road at the Peralta Trailhead. GPS: N111° 23.83' W111° 20.89'

The Hike

Start off by hiking the Dutchmans Trail east over a low ridge. The trail continues east along the foothills, then passes Miners Needle with its multiple summits. At the junction with the Coffee Flat Trail, turn northwest (left). The trail climbs up to Miners Summit via several switchbacks and meets the Whiskey Spring Trail at this pass. Now the trail descends a broad drainage toward the imposing cliffs of Bluff Spring Mountain.

At the base of the mountain, turn left onto the Bluff Spring Trail. Crystal Spring is located at this trail junction. The Bluff Spring Trail heads west and climbs gradually up Bluff Spring Canyon to a pass, then turns south and descends a tributary of Barks Canyon. Stay left at the Terrapin Trail junction and remain on the Bluff Spring Trail, continuing across Barks Canyon. This is an especially scenic area of cliffs and pinnacles, and the canyon often has flowing water during the cool season. The trail climbs south out of the canyon, swings around a ridge, then descends to Peralta Trailhead.

Bluff Spring Loop

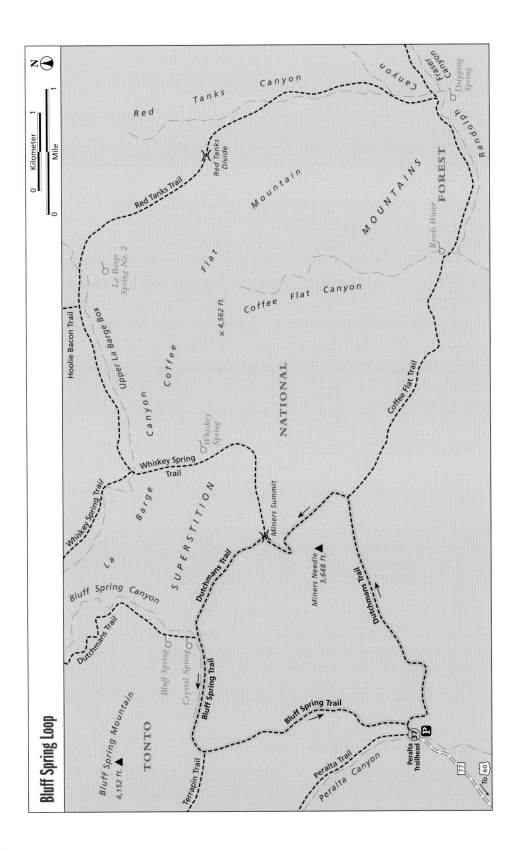

N

Kilometer
0   1

Mile
0   1

Red   Tanks   Canyon

Fraser Canyon

Dripping Spring

Red Tanks Divide

Red Tanks Trail

Mountain

Randolph Canyon

La Barge Spring No. 2

Hoolie Bacon Trail

Upper La Barge Box

Coffee

Flat

Coffee Flat Canyon

FOREST

MOUNTAINS

Reeds Water

x 4,562 ft.

Canyon

Whiskey Spring

Whiskey Spring Trail

Whiskey Spring Trail

NATIONAL

SUPERSTITION

Barge

Miners Summit

Coffee Flat Trail

La

Dutchmans Trail

Miners Needle
3,648 ft.

Bluff Spring Canyon

Dutchmans Trail

Dutchmans Trail

Bluff Spring

Crystal Spring

Bluff Spring Trail

TONTO

Bluff Spring Mountain
4,152 ft.

Terrapin Trail

Bluff Spring Trail

Peralta Trail

Peralta Canyon

Peralta Canyon

Peralta Trailhead

37

P

77

To 60

Miles and Directions

0.0 Begin at Peralta Trailhead.

2.4 Coffee Flat Trail junction; stay left.

3.5 Miners Summit/Whiskey Spring Trail junction; stay left.

4.6 Bluff Spring Trail junction; turn left.

5.7 Terrapin Trail junction; keep left.

7.7 Return to Peralta Trailhead.

NO GOLD IN THEM THAR HILLS

You can see several old mines and prospect holes along the cliffs of Bluff Spring Mountain. Stories of a lost gold mine once drew hordes of prospectors to the Superstition Mountains. Up until about 1970, the Bluff Spring Mountain and Weavers Needle areas were fiercely contested by gold-seekers, in spite of the fact the most of the Superstition Mountains are composed of relatively young volcanic rocks, which are not known for gold-bearing deposits. The Forest Service finally put an end to the destructive prospecting by withdrawing the area from mineral location.

38 Dutchmans Loop

This loop hike is very popular, and for good reason. It stays on well-graded, good trails throughout, yet passes through a variety of scenic terrain in the western Superstition Mountains. Highlights include the pinnacles of Miners Needle; the towering triple summits of the Superstition Mountains' most famous landmark, Weavers Needle; and the "stone ghosts"—volcanic stone hoodoos—of upper East Boulder Canyon and Peralta Canyon. It is an especially good introduction to backpacking for those new to the sport.

Start: About 17 miles southeast of Apache Junction

Distance: 16.2-mile loop

Approximate hiking time: 10 hours or 2 days

Elevation change: 3,330 feet

Difficulty: Moderate due to length and elevation change

Seasons: Fall through spring

Trail surface: Dirt and rocks

Water: Crystal Spring, Bluff Spring, La Barge Spring, Charlebois Spring, White Rock Spring

Other trail users: Horses

Land status: Superstition Wilderness, Tonto National Forest

Nearest town: Apache Junction

Fees and permits: Group size limited to 15; stay limit 14 days.

Maps: USGS Weavers Needle; Trail Illustrated Superstition and Four Peaks Wildernesses; USFS Superstition Wilderness, USFS Tonto National Forest

Trail contact: Mesa Ranger District, Tonto National Forest

Finding the trailhead: From Apache Junction, drive about 8.5 miles east on U.S. Highway 60, then turn left onto Peralta Road (Forest Road 77), which is maintained dirt. Continue 8 miles to the end of the road at the Peralta Trailhead. GPS: N111° 23.83' W111° 20.89'

The Hike

Hike east on the Dutchmans Trail over a low ridge. The trail loops around the base of Miners Needle, passing the junction with the Coffee Flat Trail, and then climbs to Miners Summit via a couple of switchbacks. It then descends northwest to Crystal Spring at the base of Bluff Spring Mountain. Turning northeast, the good trail descends Bluff Spring Canyon, passing the spur trail to Bluff Spring, then turns more to the north and works its way down to La Barge Canyon and the junction with the Red Tanks Trail. La Barge Spring is located just east of this junction on the north side of the canyon.

Stay left on the Dutchmans Trail and follow it down La Barge Canyon to the northwest. A spur trail leads to Music Canyon Spring. At the junction with the Peters Trail, you can reach Charlebois Spring by following the Peters Trail a short distance into the side canyon. The main trail continues down La Barge

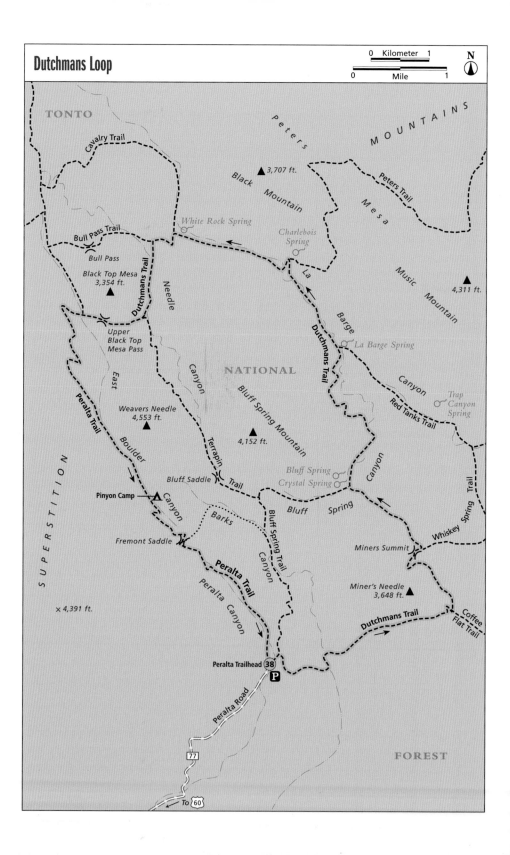

Dutchmans Loop

0   Kilometer   1

0   Mile   1

N

TONTO

Peters

MOUNTAINS

Cavalry Trail

▲ 3,707 ft.

Black

Peters Trail

Mountain

Mesa

White Rock Spring

Charlebois
Spring

Bull Pass Trail

La

Music

Bull Pass

Needle

Mountain

▲ 4,311 ft.

Black Top Mesa
3,354 ft.
▲

Dutchmans Trail

Barge

Upper
Black Top
Mesa Pass

NATIONAL

Dutchmans Trail

La Barge Spring

Canyon

East

Canyon

Bluff Spring Mountain

Trap
Canyon
Spring

Peralta Trail

Boulder

Weavers Needle
4,553 ft.
▲

▲
4,152 ft.

Red Tanks Trail

Canyon

Terrapin Trail

Bluff Spring
Crystal Spring

SUPERSTITION

Bluff Saddle

Whiskey Spring Trail

Pinyon Camp △

Canyon

Barks

Bluff   Spring

Fremont Saddle

Bluff Spring Trail
Canyon

Miners Summit

Peralta Trail

Miner's Needle
3,648 ft. ▲

× 4,391 ft.

Peralta Canyon

Dutchmans Trail

Coffee
Flat Trail

Peralta Trailhead (38)

P

Peralta Road

(77)

FOREST

← To (60)

Canyon to Marsh Valley and the junction with the Cavalry Trail. White Rock Spring usually has water.

Again, stay left on the Dutchmans Trail and climb west to a low saddle. Here, at the junction with the Bull Pass Trail, the Dutchmans Trail turns south and drops into Needle Canyon. After following Needle Canyon for a while, turn right at the junction with the Terrapin Trail and follow the Dutchmans Trail up an unnamed drainage south of Black Top Mesa. The trail reaches Upper Black Top Mesa Pass, then descends northwest into East Boulder Canyon to meet the Peralta Trail. This scenic basin is dominated by towering Weavers Needle to the south. You can sometimes find water in the bed of the wash.

Turn left onto the Peralta Trail, which climbs west in well-graded switchbacks to the ridge south of Palomino Mountain, then heads south on the slopes above a tributary of Little Boulder Canyon. A few switchbacks take the trail over a saddle next to a rock outcrop, then the trail descends back into East Boulder Canyon below triple-summited Weavers Needle. It then works its way up the scenic head of East Boulder Canyon, past heavily used Pinyon Camp. Water can sometimes be found in the creek bed nearby, but you should avoid camping in this overused area. Now, via a couple of switchbacks, the Peralta Trail climbs to Fremont Saddle, then descends scenic Peralta Canyon to the Peralta Trailhead.

Miles and Directions

0.0 Begin at Peralta Trailhead.

2.4 Coffee Flat Trail junction; continue left.

3.5 Miners Summit/Whiskey Spring Trail junction; stay left.

4.6 Bluff Spring Trail junction; keep right on Dutchmans Trail.

6.6 Red Tanks Trail junction and La Barge Spring; stay left.

7.7 Peters Trail and Charlebois Spring; stay left.

8.9 Marsh Valley, White Rock Spring, and Cavalry Trail; stay left.

9.2 Bull Pass Trail junction; stay left.

10.0 Terrapin Trail junction; turn right.

10.8 Peralta Trail in East Boulder Canyon; turn left onto Peralta Trail.

14.4 Cross Fremont Saddle.

16.2 Return to Peralta Trailhead.

GREEN TIP

Be courteous of others. Many people visit natural areas for quiet, peace, and solitude, so avoid making loud noises and intruding on others' privacy.

THE YUCCA

Yucca plants grow throughout the western Superstition Mountains. There are several varieties, but they all feature a base of slender, stiff, sharp-tipped leaves that point out in all directions, and a tall central stalk that appears when the plant flowers. Each species of yucca has its own interdependent moth, which pollinates that species of yucca and no other. Yuccas were important to Native Americans, who ate the fruits and made baskets from the tough fibers.

Most species of yuccca have long, narrow leaves growing from their base or main stem.

39 Barks Canyon

For those hikers who want a taste of the possibilities opened up by cross-country, off-trail hiking, this loop is a great place to start. Highlights include scenic Peralta Canyon and Fremont Saddle, famous for their towering rhyolite pinnacles—the "stone ghosts" of the Superstition Mountains—and the classic view of Weavers Needle. The cross-country portion of the hike follows Barks Canyon downstream to meet a good trail, so navigation is simple.

Start: About 17 miles southeast of Apache Junction

Distance: 4.6-mile loop

Approximate hiking time: 4–5 hours

Elevation change: 1,880 feet

Difficulty: Moderate due to cross-country section

Seasons: Fall through spring

Trail surface: Dirt and rocks

Water: None

Other trail users: Horses

Land status: Superstition Wilderness, Tonto National Forest

Nearest town: Apache Junction

Fees and permits: Group size limited to 15; stay limit 14 days.

Maps: USGS Weavers Needle; Trail Illustrated Superstition and Four Peaks Wildernesses; USFS Superstition Wilderness, USFS Tonto National Forest

Trail contact: Mesa Ranger District, Tonto National Forest

Finding the trailhead: From Apache Junction, drive about 8.5 miles east on U.S. Highway 60, then turn left onto Peralta Road (Forest Road 77), which is maintained dirt. Continue 8 miles to the end of the road at the Peralta Trailhead. GPS: N111° 23.83' W111° 20.89'

The Hike

Start the loop on the well-graded Peralta Trail, which heads northwest up Peralta Canyon, climbing steadily. The trail generally stays near the bed of the canyon, occasionally crossing it. Numerous pinnacles, known locally as "stone ghosts," are scattered along the canyon and its rims. The pinnacles, composed of rhyolite, a volcanic rock, were created as erosion followed cracks through the rock and carved out odd-looking fins and pinnacles. The trail steepens somewhat near the head of Peralta Canyon, and a few short switchbacks lead to Fremont Saddle.

The Peralta Trail continues north from the saddle, but our loop heads cross-country onto the broken plateau northeast of the saddle. You'll need the topographic map and skill in cross-country route finding to follow this route. Continue northeast, then north across the plateau to its northern rim and a panoramic view of Weavers Needle. Pick your way off the rim (it's easier to the south, along the east rim), then follow the drainage northeast into Barks Canyon. The exact point at which you start the descent is not critical, because the entire eastern rim drains into Barks Canyon.

Weavers Needle is the most prominent landmark in the western Superstition Mountains.

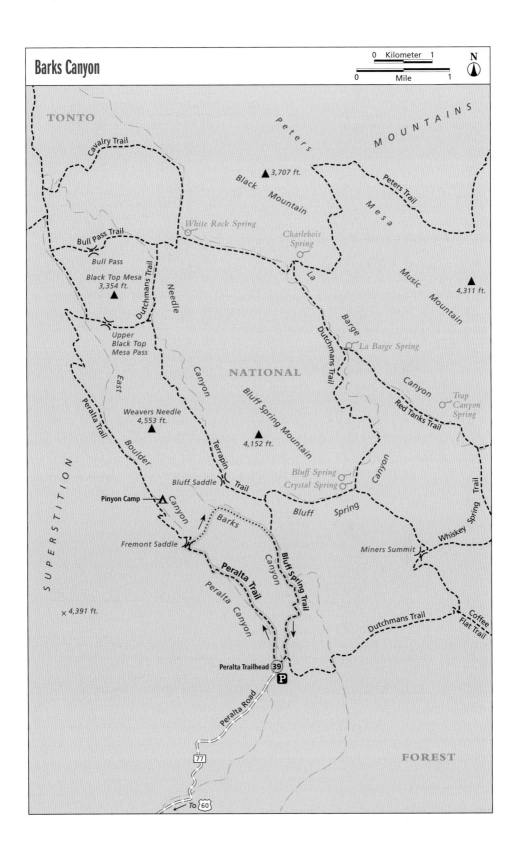

Barks Canyon

0 Kilometer 1

0 Mile 1

N

TONTO

Cavalry Trail

Peters

MOUNTAINS

Black Mountain

▲ 3,707 ft.

Peters Trail

Mesa

White Rock Spring

Charlebois Spring

Bull Pass Trail

Bull Pass

La

Music Mountain

▲ 4,311 ft.

Black Top Mesa
3,354 ft.
▲

Dutchmans Trail

Needle

Upper Black Top Mesa Pass

Barge

La Barge Spring

NATIONAL

Canyon

Dutchmans Trail

Canyon

East

Trap Canyon Spring

Red Tanks Trail

Peralta Trail

Weavers Needle
4,553 ft.
▲

Bluff Spring Mountain

▲ 4,152 ft.

Boulder

Terrapin Trail

Bluff Saddle

Bluff Spring
Crystal Spring

Canyon

Whiskey Spring Trail

Pinyon Camp △

Canyon

Barks

Bluff Spring

Canyon

Bluff Spring Trail

Fremont Saddle

Miners Summit

Peralta Trail

× 4,391 ft.

Peralta Canyon

Canyon

Dutchmans Trail

Coffee Flat Trail

SUPERSTITION

Peralta Trailhead 39

P

Peralta Road

77

FOREST

← To 60

FAMOUS NAMESAKE

Fremont Saddle is one of many places throughout the American West named for John C. Fremont, the noted American explorer who led several government-sponsored survey trips.

Now turn right and follow Barks Canyon downstream. Volcanic pinnacles and stone grottos line both sides of the shallow canyon, and it's an interesting area to explore. After a major tributary joins from the left, watch for the Bluff Spring Trail, which descends the eastern slopes into Barks Canyon. Turn right and follow this good trail back to the Peralta Trailhead.

Miles and Directions

0.0 Begin at Peralta Trailhead.

1.8 Cross Fremont Saddle.

2.0 Reach plateau rim and views of Weavers Needle.

2.6 Barks Canyon; turn right, downstream.

3.0 Bluff Spring Trail junction; turn right.

4.6 Return to Peralta Trailhead.

40 Needle Canyon

This day hike loops around all sides of the most famous Superstition Wilderness landmark, Weavers Needle. The trail through Needle Canyon takes you beneath the towering cliffs of the east face of Weavers Needle. Upper East Boulder Canyon, Fremont Pass, and Peralta Canyon have the finest display of volcanic rhyolite towers in the Superstition Mountains.

Start: About 17 miles southeast of Apache Junction

Distance: 10.6-mile loop

Approximate hiking time: 7 hours

Elevation change: 3,300 feet

Difficulty: Moderate due to length and elevation change

Seasons: Fall through spring

Trail surface: Dirt and rocks

Water: Seasonal in Barks Canyon, Needle Canyon, and East Boulder Canyon

Other trail users: Horses

Land status: Superstition Wilderness, Tonto National Forest

Nearest town: Apache Junction

Fees and permits: Group size limited to 15; stay limit 14 days.

Maps: USGS Goldfield and Weavers Needle; Trail Illustrated Superstition and Four Peaks Wildernesses; USFS Superstition Wilderness, USFS Tonto National Forest

Trail contact: Mesa Ranger District, Tonto National Forest

Finding the trailhead: From Apache Junction, drive about 8.5 miles east on U.S. Highway 60, then turn left onto Peralta Road (Forest Road 77), which is maintained dirt. Continue 8 miles to the end of the road at the Peralta Trailhead. GPS: N111° 23.83' W111° 20.89'

The Hike

From the trailhead, start out on the Bluff Spring Trail and follow the well-graded trail across Barks Canyon. The trail climbs 1.4 miles north up a tributary of Barks Canyon to meet the Terrapin Trail; turn left here. A gradual climb to the northwest leads to Bluff Saddle. The triple summits of Weavers Needle dominate the view to the northwest, and the cliffs of Bluff Spring Mountain tower above you on the east.

After Bluff Saddle, the trail descends gradually into the drainage of Needle Canyon, working its way generally north-northwest through complex country. It climbs a bit to reach Terrapin Pass, then descends north into Needle Canyon and ends at the Dutchmans Trail. Turn left here and follow the Dutchmans Trail over Upper Black Top Mesa Pass and down to East Boulder Canyon, where there is seasonal water. Turn left onto the Peralta Trail to return to the trailhead (see the Dutchmans Loop hike for details on this section).

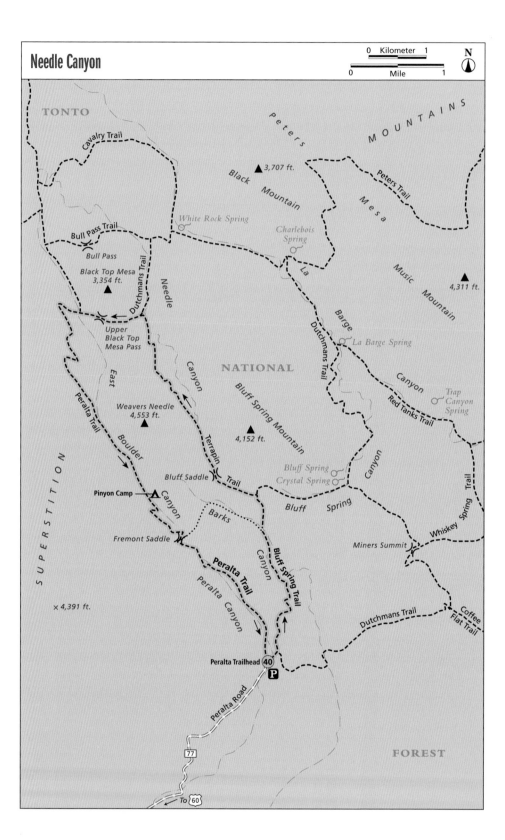

Needle Canyon

0   Kilometer   1

0   Mile   1

N

TONTO

Peters

MOUNTAINS

Cavalry Trail

Black Mountain

▲ 3,707 ft.

Peters Trail

Mesa

Bull Pass Trail

White Rock Spring

Charlebois Spring

Music Mountain

▲ 4,311 ft.

Bull Pass

Black Top Mesa
3,354 ft. ▲

Dutchmans Trail

Needle

La

Barge

Upper
Black Top
Mesa Pass

La Barge Spring

Dutchmans Trail

Canyon

East

Canyon

NATIONAL

Bluff Spring Mountain

Canyon

Red Tanks Trail

Trap
Canyon
Spring

Peralta Trail

Weavers Needle
4,553 ft. ▲

▲ 4,152 ft.

Boulder

Terrapin Trail

Bluff Spring
Crystal Spring

Canyon

Bluff Saddle

Pinyon Camp △

Canyon

Barks

Bluff   Spring

Whiskey Spring Trail

SUPERSTITION

Fremont Saddle

Peralta Trail

Bluff Spring Trail

Miners Summit

× 4,391 ft.

Peralta Canyon

Canyon

Dutchmans Trail

Coffee
Flat Trail

Peralta Trailhead (40)

P

Peralta Road

77

To 60

FOREST

Weavers Needle is the central landmark of the western Superstition Mountains.

DUTCHMAN'S LAST LAUGH

The Weavers Needle area is alleged to be the location of the fabulous Lost Dutchman Gold Mine. The "Dutchman" was actually Jacob Waltz, a German immigrant who apparently did have a gold mine somewhere, because he was seen returning to Phoenix with pack-saddles full of gold ore. Unscrupulous people attempted to follow Waltz back to his mine, but he would lead them on wild-goose chases through the mountains near Phoenix and often through the Superstition Mountains. Waltz died in Phoenix in 1891, but not before whispering to a neighbor that his rich gold mine was located where the shadow of Weavers Needle fell at 4:00 p.m. There are a couple of major problems with this statement. First, he didn't specify a date, and over the course of a year the tip of the shadow covers dozens of square miles of extremely rugged country. And second, the Superstitions do not consist of gold-bearing rocks. His mine was probably located in the Goldfield or Mazatzal Mountains. It seems likely that the Dutchman's statement was a final joke on the greedy people who had been trying to steal his mine. If so, it was wildly successful—thousands of people have scoured the Superstitions since his death and have found nothing—except, possibly, adventure.

Miles and Directions

0.0 From Peralta Trailhead start on Bluff Spring Trail.

2.0 Terrapin Trail junction; turn left.

2.6 Cross Bluff Saddle.

3.8 Cross Terrapin Pass.

4.5 Dutchmans Trail junction; turn left.

5.0 Cross Upper Black Top Mesa Pass.

5.3 Peralta Trail junction; turn left.

8.9 Cross Fremont Saddle.

10.6 Return to Peralta Trailhead.

Appendix A: Tips for Hiking Near Phoenix

Hiking Techniques

Walking is a lost art. Walking on trails and cross-country, on surfaces that may be far from smooth and flat, is not just a matter of "picking 'em up and putting 'em down"! Learning how to walk in the backcountry adds greatly to your pleasure and endurance.

Many novice hikers try to go too fast and then find themselves out of breath and stopping frequently. The group should move at a speed that allows easy (not breathless!) conversation among all members. Long hikes, especially uphill sections, should be paced so that rest breaks are needed only about once an hour. That's not to say that you shouldn't stop at scenic viewpoints or when you find something else that is interesting. But if you find yourself taking a great many breaks, you're probably going too fast. Keep rest stops short, so you don't become chilled. It's harder to get going after a long break.

As you walk, always pay attention to the stretch immediately in front of you. Hazards such as spiny plants, overhanging sharp branches, and sunbathing rattlesnakes are easy to miss if you only have eyes for the scenery on the horizon. On the other hand, daydreaming is an important part of hiking. There are always sections of trail that aren't very interesting. Along such stretches, the experienced hiker can let his mind wander far away but still pay attention to the trail underfoot and the route ahead. Or he can focus on aspects of the environment such as birdsong or identifying trees from a distance by their general shape. Either technique lets the miles pass almost unnoticed.

Hikes taken with young children should have extremely modest goals. A day hike of a few hundred yards may be enough. Within just a small area, children find all sorts of interesting things that their parents would never notice. Seeing the natural world anew through a child's eyes is a wonderful and enlightening experience.

Equipment

A modest amount of good equipment, along with the skill and technique to use it, makes hiking safer and more enjoyable. Day hiking is very popular because it can be enjoyed with a small commitment of time and just a small selection of specialized equipment. Longer hikes require that you acquire some gear, but don't let that stop you. Spending the night in the backcountry, away from civilization, helps you really understand and enjoy wilderness. Several hikes in this book are ideally suited for first-time backpackers. You can find these in the Trail Finder. Acquiring some basic gear—a good pack, tent or other shelter, sleeping bag, and boots—shouldn't be difficult either. If you're not sure where to begin, look for local outdoor shops staffed by people who use the gear and are willing to share their knowledge with you. Such shops are a valuable resource and are worth supporting. If you can't find a good local shop, mail order and the Internet are good alternatives. Check the ads in outdoor magazines for addresses and phone numbers.

Pack

A well-fitting, well-made daypack goes a long way toward making your hike a pleasant experience. Better designs have padded shoulder straps, waistbands to prevent pack movement, and zippered pockets for storing small items that you may need frequently.

Packs for backpacking fall into two categories: internal frame and external frame. A good backpack of either type distributes the load between your shoulders, back, and hips, with much of the weight on your hips. Correct fit is critical. Avoid hand-me-down packs that are the wrong size.

Shelter

Most backpackers depend on a tent for shelter. Sound construction and high quality are important. A three-season, two-person freestanding tent is the most versatile. Some hikers avoid the weight and expense of a tent by carrying a tarp with a separate groundsheet. A tarp also makes a good sunshade for lunch stops in treeless country and is sometimes worth carrying on day hikes as well as backpack trips.

Sleeping Bag

Anyone planning to spend the night on a hike should have a lightweight backpacking sleeping bag. With a good sleeping bag, you'll most likely have a comfortable sleep; a poor bag will guarantee a miserable experience. The occasional user will probably be happy with a backpacker-style mummy bag insulated with one of the current synthetic fills. People who do extended backpack trips often prefer down bags because of their lighter weight and easier packing. Sleeping bags are rated by temperature and sometimes by recommended seasons. Remember, some people sleep colder than others—if that's the case, buy a warmer bag.

Sleeping Pad

Since lightweight sleeping bags don't provide much insulation or padding underneath the sleeper, you'll need a sleeping pad. Closed-cell foam pads are cheap and durable, but not very comfortable. Air mattresses have fallen out of favor among desert hikers because they seem to attract cactus spines like a magnet. Self-inflating foam pads are both comfortable and warm, and because they are inflated to lower pressures than air mattresses, don't seem to be as likely to puncture. Still, always use a groundsheet or a tent floor, and check carefully for cactus spines. And carry a repair kit.

Mohave rattlesnakes on the trail in the Mazatzal Mountains aren't always so obvious!

Boots

For short easy hikes on good trails, nearly any comfortable footwear such as tennis shoes or running shoes will work. For difficult hiking with heavy loads, some hikers prefer all leather boots. Other experienced hikers prefer lightweight boots or low-cut hiking shoes even for very difficult cross-country hiking.

Good quality, well-fitting socks are critical to hiking comfort. A good combination is a light inner sock of cotton, wool, or synthetic fiber with a medium or heavyweight outer sock made of wool with nylon reinforcing. The outer sock will tend to slide on the inner sock, rather than directly on your skin, reducing the chance of blisters. Incipient blisters should be treated before they happen. A hot spot can be protected with a piece of felt moleskin. Often a change of socks will help as well.

Many hikers find a walking stick helpful, especially at stream crossings and on rough trails or terrain. Some hikers use a pair of "trekking poles," though having both hands occupied with walking sticks makes use of cameras and binoculars awkward. If you want to see wildlife, avoid metal-tipped poles. Most walking sticks and trekking poles have a rubber tip option, which not only is quieter but grips better on rocky Arizona trails.

Other Equipment Essentials

On all hikes that are more than a casual stroll, you should carry certain essentials. Besides water and food, for which you'll find tips below, don't forget rain/wind gear, sunglasses, sunscreen, knife, lighter or other reliable fire starter, map, compass, and a flashlight. These items can easily be carried in a small fanny pack and may save your life if you are delayed or the weather suddenly changes.

First-Aid Kit

You should always carry at least a small first-aid kit. On backpack trips, you'll need a larger, more complete kit, but the weight of the first-aid kit and other communal gear can be shared among the group. Make sure your first-aid kit is intended specifically for wilderness sports. And take a first-aid class. Knowledge is your best defense.

Clothing

Nearly any durable clothing will do for hiking in good, stable weather. On hot, sunny days, keep your skin covered and use a good sunscreen. Long pants will also protect your skin from scratches when you're hiking a brushy trail.

Use the layer system when hiking in cold or stormy weather. The layer system saves weight and bulk, because layers can be combined as needed. In cold, wet weather, the four-layer system works well: The inner layer consists of lightweight, synthetic, wicking long underwear; the next layer consists of sturdy pants and a sturdy shirt that will hold up to brush and rocks; the third layer consists of an insulating jacket or parka; and the fourth layer is your rain gear.

Don't put up with being overheated or chilled while hiking. Stop to add or subtract layers as necessary to stay comfortable.

Food

You should bring some food on all but the shortest hikes. High-calorie food keeps your energy level high. Make sandwiches or bring fruit, cheese, crackers, nuts, and drink mixes.

Backpackers have to plan their food more carefully, keeping weight and bulk to a minimum. Dehydrated foods eliminate the weight of unnecessary water. Some suggestions for a backpacker's breakfast include low-bulk cold cereals with powdered milk, hot cereals, dried fruit, breakfast bars, hot chocolate, tea, and coffee bags. For lunch, try munchies such as nuts, cheese, crackers, dried fruit, candy bars, athletic energy bars, dried soup, hard candy, beef or turkey jerky, sardines, and fruit-flavored drink mixes. For dinner, try dried noodle or rice-based dishes supplemented with margarine or olive oil, and a small package of tuna, turkey, or chicken.

Water

On day hikes, bring water from home. Water is the most important item in your pack—be sure you have enough. Each hiker may drink a gallon or more during a long, difficult hike, and hot weather greatly increases the amount of water you'll need. On backpack trips, you will have to use water from wilderness springs, streams, or lakes; always purify it with a proven water purification system (see Water Essentials under Making It a Safe Trip).

Camping

Choose campsites on durable, naturally drained surfaces such as forest duff, sand, gravel, or rock slabs. If you're camping in the forest, look above you for dead branches that could break off. Avoid fragile meadows and sites next to springs and creeks. Never dig drainage ditches or make other "improvements." Rangers sometimes must close specific areas to camping or entry to allow them to recover from heavy use.

Campfires

Don't build campfires except in an emergency. There are far too many fire scars in Arizona's backcountry. If you have warm clothing and a good sleeping bag, you'll be warmer without a fire.

Campfires are prohibited in certain areas and during periods of high fire danger. Check with the land management agency listed with each hike for current regulations. Don't ever build a fire on a windy day, and always put your fire out completely

Stunning flowers grow from otherwise obscure hedgehog cactus.

by mixing the coals with water or dirt until the ashes are cool to the touch. Most of the recent large wildfires in Arizona were caused by campers who failed to extinguish their campfire. Do you really want to be the person who burned hundreds of square miles of beautiful forest and killed all that wildlife?

Trash

If you carried it in, you can also carry it out. Never bury food or trash. Animals will always dig it up and scatter it. Don't feed wild creatures because they easily develop a dependency on human food, which can lead to unpleasant encounters and cause the animal to starve during the off-season.

Sanitation

A short walk in any popular recreation area or along a roadside proves that few people seem to know how to answer the call of nature away from facilities. Diseases such as giardiasis are spread by poor human sanitation. If facilities are available, use them. In the backcountry, select a site at least 100 yards from streams, lakes, springs, and dry washes. Avoid barren, sandy soil, if possible. Next, dig a small "cat-hole" about 6 inches down into the organic layer of the soil. (Some people carry a small plastic trowel for this purpose.) When finished, refill the hole, covering any toilet paper. In many areas, regulations require that you carry out used toilet paper.

Trail Courtesy

Don't cut switchbacks. It takes more effort than staying on the trail and also increases erosion and destroys trails. Give horses pack animals the right-of-way by stepping off the trail on the downhill side and standing quietly. Follow any instructions given by the rider. You will encounter mountain bikes outside designated wilderness areas. Even though hikers have the right-of-way over bikes, it's easy to step aside so the riders can pass without having to veer off the trail and make ruts.

It is illegal to smoke while hiking or riding in the national forest. Smokers must stop at a bare spot or rock ledge, then make certain that all smoking materials are out before continuing. During periods of high fire danger, all fires, including charcoal, campfires, and smoking, may be prohibited on public lands.

Although dogs are allowed in national forests and designated wilderness areas, it is your responsibility to keep them from bothering wildlife or other hikers. In some state parks, dogs are not allowed on trails. In the Tonto National Forests, dogs must be kept under control and on a leash when required.

Don't cut live trees or plants of any kind, carve on trees or rocks, pick wildflowers, or build rock campfire rings, prayer circles, or other structures. Leave the wilderness as you found it.

Motorized vehicles and bicycles, including mountain bikes and electric bikes, are prohibited in all designated wilderness areas. State parks and other areas have their own restrictions.

Making It a Safe Trip

Wilderness is not inherently dangerous, just indifferent. You can make it a safe place if you are willing to respect your limitations and always work with the conditions at hand. You can safely gain confidence and self-reliance if you start out with easy hikes and progress to more difficult adventures. Keep learning, and you will find that being on your own in the backcountry, whether for a day or a week, is a deeply satisfying experience. After all, it's the environment we evolved in, not our modern urban civilization with all its complexities.

Trip Planning

Individuals or parties pushing too hard often suffer backcountry accidents. Instead, set reasonable goals, allowing for delays caused by weather, deteriorated trails, unexpectedly rough country, and dry springs. Remember that the group must move at the speed of the slowest member. Be flexible enough to eliminate part of a hike if your original plans appear too ambitious. Do not fall into the trap of considering a trip plan "cast in stone"—rather, take pride in your adaptability. Plan your trip carefully using maps, guidebooks, and information from reliable sources such as experienced hikers and backcountry rangers.

When backpacking, consider alternatives to traditional campsites. Dry camping—that is, camping away from water sources—virtually eliminates the possibility of

Much smaller than mountain lions, bobcats pose no danger to hikers unless cornered. These two are at the Arizona Sonora Desert Museum.

contaminating wilderness streams and springs. You can also avoid heavily used camp-sites and their camp-robbing animal attendants such as skunks, mice, rock squirrels, jays, and insects, and enjoy beautiful, uncrowded campsites. The technique is simple: Use a collapsible water container to pick up water at the last reliable source of the day, keeping going for an hour or so until you find that perfect campsite with the stunning view, and then use minimum water for camp chores. With practice it will become second nature.

Water Essentials

Backcountry water sources are not safe to drink. Infections from contaminated water are uncomfortable and can be disabling. Giardiasis, for example, is a severe gastrointestinal infection caused by small cysts, which can result in an emergency evacuation of the infected hiker. Purify all backcountry water sources. Halogen-based tablets are the most effective and lightweight purifying method (see Medicine for Mountaineering, in Further Reading). Water filters are popular, but few of them kill viruses. The term "water purifier" usually means a filter with an active iodine element that kills viruses. You can also purify water by bringing it to a rolling boil. This produces safe water at any altitude. Afterward, pour the water back and forth between containers to cool it and improve its taste.

Backcountry Navigation

Maps

Maps are essential for finding your way in the backcountry. Don't depend on trail signs, which are sometimes missing.

Topographic maps are the most useful for backcountry navigation because they show the elevation and shape of the land. All of Arizona is covered by the 7.5-minute quadrangle series published by the US Geological Survey, which are the most accurate maps available for showing natural features. Unfortunately, USGS topo maps are not being revised very often, which means that man-made features such as roads and trails are often out-of-date. Each hike description in this book lists the USGS topographic maps that cover the hike.

The USDA Forest Service and several private companies publish recreational and wilderness area topographic maps with more up-to-date trail information. The most useful of these in the area covered by this book are the US Forest Service Superstition and Mazatzal Wilderness maps, and the National Geographic Trails Illustrated maps. These maps are listed under maps for each hike, if available. The US Forest Service also publishes national forest road maps that are useful for finding the trailhead—these maps are listed if available.

Web and app-based maps are now available that make trip planning and just plain day dreaming about the backcountry a pleasure you can enjoy on your computer, tablet, or phone. Trip planning tools let you measure trail distances and create routes and waypoints for GPS. And you can share your trip with friends or the public. You can also print custom maps for your hike. Currently, my two favorites are CalTopo .com and GaiaGPS.com.

Before entering the backcountry, study the maps to become familiar with the general lay of the land. This is a good time to establish a baseline, a long, unmistakable landmark such as a road or highway that borders the area. In the rare event that you become totally disoriented, you can always use your compass to follow a general course toward your baseline. Although hiking to your baseline will probably take you out of your way, it's comforting to always know you can find a route back to known country.

In the desert mountains and Central Highlands, remember that cross-country travel is usually easiest along high terrain such as ridges. Although desert washes may appear to be obvious routes, the soft sand and gravel drag at your feet and create slow going. In the mountains, canyon bottoms are often choked with brush and boulders and have dry waterfalls; deep, cold pools; and other hidden obstacles.

While hiking, refer to the map often and locate yourself in reference to visible landmarks. Use trail signs to confirm your location. If you do this consistently, you will never become lost.

GPS

The satellite-based Global Positioning System is very useful in areas where landmarks are few, such as pinyon-juniper flats, dense forest, canyons, and when bad weather hides landmarks. Though GPS makes it possible to find your location nearly anywhere, a GPS receiver is no substitute for a good map and a reliable compass. With GPS alone, you will know your coordinates, but without a map such coordinates are just a bunch of meaningless numbers. Without a compass you won't know which way to travel. As with any mechanical or electronic device, it can fail. Bring spare batteries.

GPS works especially well in combination with computer-based topographic maps. Several companies produce regional and statewide coverage, usually based on the government topo maps but enhanced with more up-to-date data. With computer maps, you can plot GPS waypoints on the computer and then download them to your GPS receiver. You can also use a variety of onscreen tools to measure distances and elevations, which can be of great help planning your hike. You can then print custom maps for your trip.

The GPS coordinates in this book use the lat/log system and the WGS 84 datum. Be sure to set your GPS receiver accordingly before using the coordinates in this book.

Weather

During the summer, heat is a hazard at lower elevations. In hot weather, each hiker will need a gallon or more of water every day. To avoid dehydration, drink more water

It takes a specific combination of temperature, light, and soil chemistry and composition to coax desert wildflower seeds to bloom.

than required merely to quench your thirst. Sport drinks, which replace electrolytes, are very useful. Eating a small amount of salty food, such as nuts, is also helpful in replacing salts lost through heavy exercise.

Protection both from the heat and the sun is important: wear a lightweight sun hat and use sunscreen rate at least SPF 15. During hot weather, hike in the mountains at higher elevations, or hike early in the day to avoid the afternoon heat.

Thunderstorms, which bring high wind, heavy rain and hail, and lightning, may occur at any time of year but are common from July through September. When thunderstorms form, stay off exposed ridges and mountaintops and away from lone trees.

Hypothermia is a life-threatening condition caused by continuous exposure to chilling weather. Rainy, windy weather causes an insidious heat loss and is especially dangerous. Snowfall and blizzard conditions can occur at any time of year in the higher mountains. Hypothermia may be prevented by adjusting your clothing layers to avoid chilling or overheating, and by eating and drinking regularly so that your body continues to produce heat. In severe conditions, get out of the wet weather as soon as you can, by camping early or cutting your day hike short.

Insects and Their Kin

A few desert mosquitoes sometimes appear after wet spring weather but aren't generally a problem. Although most scorpions can inflict a painful sting, only the small, straw-colored scorpion found in the lower deserts is dangerous. Black widow and brown recluse spiders can also be a hazard, especially to young children and adults who are allergic. Susceptible individuals should carry insect sting kits prescribed by their doctors. Kissing bugs and other obnoxious insects are dormant during cool weather but are active in warm weather. Use a net tent to keep nighttime prowlers away when camping in warm weather in the deserts. You can avoid most scorpion and spider encounters by never placing your hands or bare feet where you can't see. Kick over rocks and logs before picking them up.

Aggressive Africanized bees are found throughout the state and are indistinguishable from domesticated honeybees. The best way to avoid being stung is to give all bees a wide berth. If attacked, drop your pack, protect your eyes, and head for dense brush, or a building or vehicle if one is nearby.

Snakes

Arizona boasts more species of rattlesnakes than any other state—eleven species and several varieties. Rattlesnakes are most common at lower elevations but may be encountered anywhere. Since rattlesnakes can strike no farther than approximately half their body length, avoid placing your hands and feet in areas that you cannot see, and walk several feet away from rock overhangs and shady ledges. Because bites often occur on feet, ankle-high hiking boots and loose-fitting long pants will help. Snakes, which are cold-blooded, prefer surfaces at about 80 degrees F, so during hotter weather watch for snakes in shady places. In cool weather be alert for sunning snakes on open ground.

No fatalities have been attributed to the bite of the venomous Gila monster, but they can bite quickly and they hold on tight. This one was photographed in the Mazatzal Mountains.

Wildlife

Wild animals normally leave you alone unless molested or provoked. Black bears, mountain lions, wolves, and coyotes are far less dangerous than the texting drivers you'll encounter on the way to the trailhead. Never, ever feed any wild animal, as they rapidly get accustomed to handouts and then will vigorously defend their new food source. And then they'll starve to death during the off season when humans are gone. Around camp, problems with rodents can be avoided by hanging your food from rocks or trees.

Plants

Poison ivy grows along streams and dry washes at intermediate elevations. The leaves, stems, and berries of poison ivy are poisonous to the touch. The plant is easily recognized by its leaves, which grow in groups of three. Contact causes a rash, which later starts to blister. Unless large areas of skin are involved, or the reaction is severe, no specific treatment is required. If you suspect contact with poison ivy, wash immediately with soap and water, if available. Calamine lotion will relieve the itching.

Cactus and other spiny plants occur at all elevations in this area. Some cacti, especially cholla, have tiny barbs on their spines, which cause the burrs to cling ferociously. Use a pair of sticks to quickly and carefully pluck the burr or joint from your skin or clothing. A pair of tweezers is essential for removing spines.

Never eat any wild plant, unless you know its identity. Many common plants, especially mushrooms, are deadly.

Rescue

Anyone entering remote country should be self-sufficient and prepared to take care of emergencies such as equipment failure and minor medical problems. Very rarely, circumstances may create a life-threatening situation that requires a search effort or an emergency evacuation. Always leave word of your hiking plans with a reliable individual. For backpack trips, you should provide a written itinerary and a map. In your instructions, allow extra time for routine delays, and always make contact as soon as you are out. The responsible person should be advised to contact the appropriate authority if you become overdue. County sheriffs are responsible for search and rescue; you can also contact forest or park rangers.

If you have a cellular phone, it's worth trying in an emergency situation. It may work, especially if you are on a ridge or other high point. But don't count on a cell phone for communication in the backcountry. Cell phones are radios that must be within line of sight of a cellular site in order to work. Deep canyons and intervening ridges can all block the signal, and without a charger, cell phones quickly die. A far more reliable option is to carry a Personal Locator Beacon, which weighs only a couple of ounces and has a battery life of five years. A PLB is registered to the owner and transmits your precise GPS location to the search and rescue (COSPAS-SARSAT) satellite constellation, alerting the rescue authorities to your emergency within a few minutes. The appropriate search and rescue center then attempts to contact you with the information provided when you registered your PLB. If you respond and verify your emergency, or if they cannot contact you, rescuers are dispatched immediately. The COSPAS-SARSAT system is international and works everywhere on the planet, except possibly in deep slot canyons. Of course, you should never activate a PLB except in a life-threatening emergency. False activations are punishable by severe penalties.

Appendix B: Hiker Checklist

This checklist may be useful for ensuring that nothing essential is forgotten. Of course, it contains far more items than are needed on any individual hiking trip.

Clothing
- ❑ Shirt
- ❑ Pants
- ❑ Extra underwear
- ❑ Swimsuit
- ❑ Walking shorts
- ❑ Belt or suspenders
- ❑ Windbreaker
- ❑ Jacket or parka
- ❑ Rain gear
- ❑ Gloves or mittens
- ❑ Sun hat
- ❑ Watch cap or balaclava
- ❑ Sweater
- ❑ Bandanna

Footwear
- ❑ Boots
- ❑ Extra socks
- ❑ Boot wax
- ❑ Camp shoes

Sleeping Gear
- ❑ Tarp or tent with fly
- ❑ Groundsheet
- ❑ Sleeping pad
- ❑ Sleeping bag

Packs
- ❑ Backpack
- ❑ Daypack
- ❑ Fanny pack

Cooking Needs
- ❑ Matches or lighter
- ❑ Waterproof match case
- ❑ Fire starter
- ❑ Stove
- ❑ Fuel
- ❑ Stove maintenance kit
- ❑ Cooking pot(s)
- ❑ Cup
- ❑ Bowl or plate
- ❑ Utensils
- ❑ Pot scrubber
- ❑ Plastic water bottles with water
- ❑ Collapsible water containers
- ❑ Water purification tablets or filter

Food
- ❑ Cereal
- ❑ Bread
- ❑ Crackers
- ❑ Cheese
- ❑ Margarine
- ❑ Dry soup
- ❑ Packaged dinners
- ❑ Snacks
- ❑ Hot chocolate
- ❑ Tea
- ❑ Powdered milk
- ❑ Powdered drink mixes

Navigation

- ❏ Maps
- ❏ Compass
- ❏ GPS receiver

Emergency/Repair

- ❏ Personal locator beacon
- ❏ Pocketknife
- ❏ First–aid kit
- ❏ Snakebite kit
- ❏ Nylon cord
- ❏ Plastic bags
- ❏ Wallet or ID card
- ❏ Coins for phone calls
- ❏ Space blanket
- ❏ Signal mirror
- ❏ Pack parts
- ❏ Stove parts
- ❏ Tent parts
- ❏ Flashlight bulbs, batteries
- ❏ Scissors
- ❏ Safety pins

Miscellaneous

- ❏ Fishing gear
- ❏ Photographic gear
- ❏ Sunglasses
- ❏ Flashlight
- ❏ Candle lantern
- ❏ Sunscreen
- ❏ Insect repellent
- ❏ Toilet paper
- ❏ Trowel
- ❏ Binoculars
- ❏ Trash bags
- ❏ Notebook and pencils
- ❏ Field guides
- ❏ Book or game
- ❏ Dental and personal items
- ❏ Towel
- ❏ Car key
- ❏ Watch
- ❏ Calendar

Additional Supplies Stored in Vehicle

- ❏ Extra water
- ❏ Extra food
- ❏ Extra clothes

Appendix C: Agencies

City Agencies

Phoenix Parks and Recreation,
(602) 262-6862, http://phoenix.gov/parks

County Agencies

Maricopa County Parks and Recreation,
(602) 506-2930
www.maricopa.gov/parks

State Agencies

Arizona Game and Fish Department, 5000 W. Carefree Highway
Phoenix, AZ 85086-5000
(602) 942-3000
www.azgfd.com

Arizona State Land Department,
1616 W. Adams St.,
Phoenix, AZ 85007
(602) 542-4631
land.az.gov

Arizona State Parks,
23751 N. 23rd Ave., #190
Phoenix, AZ 85085, (602) 542-4174
azstateparks.com

Federal Agencies

National Forests

Tonto National Forest,
Cave Creek Ranger District,
40202 N. Cave Creek Rd.,
Scottsdale, AZ 85262, (480) 595-3300

Tonto National Forest,
Mesa Ranger District,
5140 E. Ingram St., Mesa, AZ 85205
(480) 610-3300

Tonto National Forest,
Payson Ranger District,
1009 E. Highway 260, Payson, AZ 85541, (928) 474-7900

Tonto National Forest,
Supervisors Office,
2324 E. McDowell Rd., Phoenix, AZ 85006
(602) 225-5200,
www.fs.fed.us/r3/tonto

Bureau of Land Management
Arizona State Office,
One N. Central Ave., Suite 800,
Phoenix, AZ 85004-4427
(602) 417-9200,
www.blm.gov/arizona

Phoenix District Office,
221605 N. 7th Ave.,
Phoenix, AZ 85027-2929
(623) 580-5500,
www.blm.gov/office/phoenix-district-office

Sonoran Desert National Monument,
221605 N. 7th Ave.,
Phoenix, AZ 85027-2929
(623) 580-5500
www.blm.gov/az/sonoran/sondes_main.htm

Appendix D: Clubs and Trail Groups

Arizona Mountaineering Club
http://arizonamountaineeringclub.net/

Sierra Club, Grand Canyon Chapter
http://arizona.sierraclub.org

Appendix E: Further Reading

Fletcher, Colin, and Chip Rawlins. *The Complete Walker IV.* New York: Alfred A. Knopf, 2002.

Grubbs, Bruce. *Desert Hiking Tips.* Guilford, Conn.: The Globe Pequot Press, 1999.

Harmon, Will. *Leave No Trace.* Guilford, Conn.: The Globe Pequot Press, 1997.

—*Wild Country Companion.* Guilford, Conn.: The Globe Pequot Press, 1994.

Larson, Peggy. *Sierra Club Naturalist's Guide to the Deserts of the Southwest.* San Francisco: Sierra Club Books, 2000.

Perry, John, and Jane Greverus. *Guide to the Natural Areas of New Mexico, Arizona, and Nevada.* San Francisco: Sierra Club Books, 1986.

Phillips, Steven, and Patricia Wentworth Comus, eds. *A Natural History of the Sonoran Desert.* Tucson: Arizona-Sonora Desert Museum Press, 2000.

Wilkerson, James A. *Medicine for Mountaineering.* Seattle: The Mountaineers, 2001.

Hike Index

About the Author

The author has a serious problem—he doesn't know what he wants to do when he grows up. Meanwhile, he's done such things as wildland fire fighting, running a mountain shop, flying airplanes, shooting photos, and writing books. He's a backcountry skier, climber, figure skater, mountain biker, amateur radio operator, river runner, and sea kayaker—but the thing that really floats his boat is hiking and backpacking. No matter what else he tries, the author always comes back to hiking—especially long, rough, cross-country trips in places like the Grand Canyon. Some people never learn. But what little he has learned, he's willing to share with you—via his books, of course, but also via his websites, blogs, and whatever works. He has written numerous Falcon Guides. His website is BruceGrubbs.com.